UNITED NATIONS CONFERENCE ON TRADE AND DEVELOPMENT
Geneva

ECONOMIC DEVELOPMENT IN AFRICA
REPORT 2009

STRENGTHENING
REGIONAL ECONOMIC INTEGRATION
FOR AFRICA'S DEVELOPMENT

UNITED NATIONS
New York and Geneva, 2009

NOTE

Symbols of United Nations documents are composed of capital letters combined with figures. Mention of such a symbol indicates a reference to a United Nations document.

———————————

The designations employed and the presentation of the material in this publication do not imply the expression of any opinion whatsoever on the part of the Secretariat of the United Nations concerning the legal status of any country, territory, city or area, or of its authorities, or concerning the delimitation of its frontiers or boundaries.

———————————

Material in this publication may be freely quoted or reprinted, but acknowledgement is requested, together with a reference to the document number. A copy of the publication containing the quotation or reprint should be sent to the UNCTAD secretariat.

———————————

UNCTAD/ALDC/AFRICA/2009

UNITED NATIONS PUBLICATION
Sales No. E.09.II.D.7
ISBN 978-92-1-112768-3
ISSN 1990–5114

ACKNOWLEDGEMENTS

The *Economic Development in Africa Report 2009* was prepared by a research team consisting of Norbert Lebale (team leader), Janvier Nkurunziza, Shigehisa Kasahara and Martin Halle. Melvin Ayogu and Christian Kingombe contributed as consultants.

The work was completed under the overall supervision of Charles Gore, Head, Research and Policy Analysis Branch; and Habib Ouane, Director, Division for Africa, Least Developed Countries and Special Programmes (ALDC). The report benefited from inputs provided by Masataka Fujita of the Division on Investment and Enterprise (DIAE) and from Poul Hansen, Jan Hoffmann, José Rubiato, Vincent Valentine and Birgit Viohl of the Division on Technology and Logistics (DTL). The report also benefited from the comments of the following, who participated in a peer review discussion of a draft of the Report: Dominique Njinkeu, Executive Director, International Lawyers and Economists Against Poverty (ILEAP), Bonapas Onguglo (UNCTAD) and Mehdi Shafaeddin (independent consultant).

Statistical assistance was provided by Agnès Collardeau-Angleys. Heather Wicks and Stefanie West provided secretarial support. The cover was prepared by Hadrien Gliozzo, and Michael Gibson edited the text.

The overall layout, graphics and desktop publishing were done by Madasamyraja Rajalingam.

Contents

CHAPTER 5
STRENGTHENING REGIONAL INTEGRATION IN AFRICA: SOME POLICY RECOMMENDATIONS 95

LIST OF BOXES

LIST OF FIGURES

EXPLANATORY NOTES

The $ sign refers to the United States dollar.

Sub-Saharan Africa: Except where otherwise stated, this includes South Africa.

North Africa: In this publication, Sudan is classified as part of sub-Saharan Africa, not North Africa.

Tables: Two dots (..) indicate that data are not available or are not reported separately.

ABBREVIATIONS

ACP	African, Caribbean and Pacific Group of States
AEC	African Economic Community
AGOA	African Growth and Opportunity Act (United States)
ARIA	Assessing Regional Integration in Africa (ECA)
ASEAN	Association of South-east Asian Nations
ASYCUDA	Automated System for Customs Data
AU	African Union
CEMAC	Economic and Monetary Community of Central Africa
CEN-SAD	Community of Sahel–Saharan States
CFA	Communauté financière africaine
COMESA	Common Market for Eastern and Southern Africa
EAC	East African Community
ECA	Economic Commission for Africa (United Nations)
ECCAS	Economic Community of Central African States
ECOWAS	Economic Community of West African States
EPA	economic partnership agreement
EU	European Union
FDI	foreign direct investment
FTA	free trade agreement
GATS	General Agreement on Trade in Services
GDP	gross domestic product
ICA	Infrastructure Consortium for Africa
ICTSD	International Centre for Trade and Sustainable Development
IGAD	Intergovernmental Authority on Development
IOC	Indian Ocean Commission
IOM	International Organization on Migration
LAP	Libyan Africa Portfolio for Investment
LDC	least developed country
LLDC	landlocked developing country
LPA	Lagos Plan of Action

M&A	merger and acquisition
MERCOSUR	Southern Common Market (Mercado Comun del Sur)
MIDSA	Migration Dialogue for Southern African
MIDWA	Migration Dialogue for Western Africa
NEPAD	New Partnership for African Development
OAU	Organization for African Unity
ODA	official development assistance
PTA	preferential trade agreement
RCP	regional consultative process
REC	Regional Economic Community
RTA	regional trade agreement
SACU	Southern African Customs Union
SADC	Southern African Development Community
SEATAC	Southern and Eastern African Technical ASYCUDA Centre
TICAD	Tokyo International Conference on African Development
TIDCA	Trade, Investment and Development Cooperation Agreement
TIFA	Trade and Investment Framework Agreement
TNC	transnational corporation
UEMOA	Union économique et monétaire des États de l'Afrique de l'Ouest
UMA	Arab Maghreb Union
WAEMU	West African Economic and Monetary Union
WAMZ	West African Monetary Zone
WEF	World Economic Forum
WIR	World Investment Report (UNCTAD)
WTO	World Trade Organization

INTRODUCTION

The importance of regional economic cooperation and integration as a means for accelerating and consolidating economic and social development has long been recognized by African decision-makers. Unity, cooperation and integration of Africa were long-standing aspirations of many African leaders, including George Patmore, W.E.B Dubois, Marcus Garvey, as well as African nationalists such as Kwame Nkrumah who, in his book *Africa Must Unite*, called for African unity. Hence the call for integration is well-rooted in African history, albeit, as in other regions, the initial aim was more to gain greater political clout and voice in the international arena. As the challenges of globalization and interdependence made their impact felt on the countries of the African region, including the possible marginalization of the African continent, the imperative of integration took centre stage once again. The Organization for African Unity (OAU) was established in 1963 to integrate African economies, solve conflicts within and among African countries, bring development, and improve the standard of living of Africans (Olubomehin and Kawonishe, 2004). Several African subregional groupings were subsequently formed. In June 1991, the Abuja Treaty was signed, which provided for the creation of the continent-wide African Economic Community (AEC) by 2027. The formation of regional economic cooperation arrangements serve to provide the underpinnings for the planned AEC.

Regionalism in Africa had been pursued for two reasons. The first was to enhance political unity at the pan-African level. The second was to foster economic growth and development. Regionalism, especially regional market integration, had been a way to help solve the structural problems that the African economies were confronted with.

This report will argue that strengthened intra-African integration is essential for development. Previous regional initiatives in Africa, which mainly focused on political issues, were largely seen as not having delivered much to uplift the economic conditions of its members nor ensured sustained growth. As will be elaborated on in the report, regional integration, when designed and implemented within a broader development strategy to promote economic diversification, structural changes and technological development, could enhance productive capacities of African economies, realize economies of scale and improve competitiveness and serve as a launching pad for African economies' effective participation in the global economy.

This report is topical for three reasons. First, at a time when Africa is experiencing changes in international cooperation, through its involvement in a large number of external partnerships (multilateral, regional and bilateral), it needs to exploit opportunities within the continent which could help it achieve higher economic growth rates and development objectives. Second, with the current financial and economic crisis affecting African economies through decreases in official development assistance (ODA), imports and investments, the intensification of intra-African trade offers one development strategy for trade diversification. Third, regional integration could lead to, inter alia, pooling resources and enlarging local markets for stimulating production, trade and investment. Currently, the potential of intra-African trade and investment has not been fully exploited, as seen in the low proportion of intra-African trade to total exports.

Much has been written about regional cooperation and integration in Africa. Some strands of current literature on intra-African integration deal with institutional aspects of integration. For example, the African Union and the United Nations Economic Commission for Africa have published successively three reports on *Assessing Regional Integration in Africa* (*ARIA I, ARIA II*, and *ARIA III*). These reports provide in-depth analyses of progress towards fulfilling the objectives of Africa's regional integration in broad and thematic areas, in accordance with the vision of the African Union (Economic Commission for Africa (ECA), 2008). The first edition (ECA, 2004) is a comprehensive assessment of the status of regional integration in Africa. ECA (2006a) dealt with rationalization of multiple integration groupings in Africa and their attendant overlapping memberships. ECA (2008) is focused on the theme of macroeconomic policy convergence, monetary and financial integration in Africa's Regional Economic Communities (RECs). In addition, since 2002, ECA produces an annual report on integration in Africa. The African Development Bank has produced a number of reports which revisit the issues of regional integration and cooperation in Africa, including the *African Development Report 2000: Regional Integration in Africa*. The African Development Bank report discusses the major potential benefits underpinning the rationale for regional integration in Africa, which reflects the desire to deal, in one way or another, with the perceived growth-retarding constraints inherent in small markets.

Several recent scholarly studies, including by African scholars, have assessed the record of regional integration in Africa. The African Economic Research Consortium in the late 1990s sponsored a comprehensive study on "Regional integration and trade liberalization in sub-Saharan Africa" (Oyeyide et al., 1997). This study provided an evaluation of regional integration in sub-Saharan Africa. It concentrated on economic and trade aspects as the principal field of integration. Most of these studies have focused on trade gains in the area of goods. Intra-African investments as well as trade in services and migration, which are gaining importance, have not been explored in such detail.

This report builds on these studies and aims to fill this gap in the literature. It focuses in particular on economic flows rather than institutional aspects of intra-African integration. It goes beyond the analysis of flows of trade in goods to include emerging issues such as trade in services, investment, and migration within regional integration arrangements, which have only been dealt with marginally by current studies. The objective of this year's report is to analyse the key features and pattern of intra-African regional integration in these areas, and identify some of the key opportunities that African countries could exploit or capitalize on for their development. The analysis also builds on the *Economic Development in Africa Report 2008* (UNCTAD, 2008a), particularly the role that regional integration could play in the expansion of Africa's trade following trade liberalization, as well on the issues raised in the *Trade and Development Report 2007* (UNCTAD, 2007c), which argued strongly for an approach to regional integration amongst developing countries which accelerates capital accumulation and technological progress.

The present report is organized as follows. Chapter 1 provides a brief assessment of regional integration initiatives over the past years in Africa. It describes the historical evolution in African regional integration efforts, culminating with the decision to create an African Economic Community. It also provides an assessment of regional integration initiatives in the areas of trade, investment and migration. Chapter 2 analyses intraregional trade performance in goods, the direction and composition of Africa's trade flows as well as their determinants. The chapter also provides an answer to the question whether trade flows among African economies are at their potential or whether there are prospects for expansion. Chapter 3 examines the global significance and scope of foreign direct investment (FDI) flows among African countries, the determinants, and the geographical and sectoral distribution of such flows. Chapter 4 explores intraregional performance in two emerging areas of regional integration in Africa, namely trade in services and migration. Hindrances to expand intraregional cooperation in those areas are discussed and proposals are made to improve the performance in those areas. Chapter 5 summarizes the main findings of the report and gives some policy recommendations about whether and how to meaningfully use regional economic integration for development and as a building bloc for Africa's participation and integration into the world economy.

Chapter 1

EXPERIENCE WITH REGIONAL INTEGRATION IN AFRICA: CHALLENGES AND OPPORTUNITIES

A. Theoretical justification for economic integration

Two major theoretical motivations for the formation of trade blocs are the allocation effect and the accumulation (or growth) effect of free trade within a regional bloc (Baldwin, 1997).[1] With respect to the allocation effect, economic theory shows that, in a competitive economy, the demand for a good directs productive resources to the production of that good. Hence, demand is an important signal between consumers and producers. Given that the imposition of tariff and non-tariff barriers between countries interferes with this signal, the removal of such trade barriers in the context of regional integration is thought to increase efficiency in resource allocation.

A corollary of the allocation effect is the so-called "scale and variety effects" (Baldwin, 1997). The scale effect relates to the fact that the protection of inefficient industries as seen in Africa and other developing economies during the import-substitution era maintained too many inefficient firms, many of which operated at inefficient large scales. Opening up markets in the context of an overall trade liberalization policy or within a regional trade bloc reduces this protection, which can help to rationalize entire industries through the reallocation of resources. On the other hand, by creating large markets, regional integration could allow small firms to reach their optimal size. This in turn would lower average costs, reducing consumer prices.

With respect to the variety effect, the idea is simply that integrating a country's economy into a wider market allows consumers to choose from a varied array of goods, which should increase their welfare. Increased competition across a wide range of products can also lower consumer prices. From a firm's perspective, the opportunity to choose from a wider array of production factors would enable it to use the most appropriate inputs, which could increase its productivity.

The second major effect of regionalism, that of accumulation, is observed through the investment and trade channels. When economic integration expands regional markets, more suppliers are attracted to the regional market and firms have the opportunity to specialize. This reduces average production costs within the trade bloc, increasing the return to factors of production and hence physical and non-physical (including knowledge) factor accumulation.[2] It is now largely accepted that one of the effects of globalization has been to increase the mobility of human and financial resources, which tend to flow to economies with the highest rates of return. Moreover, technological spillovers resulting from regionalism lead to increases in productivity and the reduction of production costs, further attracting more investment, and hence, factor accumulation. The combination of the effects of regional economic integration on efficiency and accumulation lead to the recognition that regional integration can have a positive effect on economic growth. Considering that higher efficiency and faster accumulation are ingredients of a competitive system, regional integration could be a stepping stone for Africa's integration in the global economy.

The formation of a trade bloc can thus have an influence on the location decisions of foreign firms. According to the new economic geography school, the three key location variables are (a) market size, (b) the cost of production and the availability of relevant production factors, and (c) market access (Krugman, 1991). Offering the most segmented market in the world, Africa's trade costs are much higher than in any other region (see table 8), which has discouraged foreign investment while keeping trade flows at very low levels. Market expansion through regional economic integration can contribute to overcoming this constraint. Moreover, free movement of capital, labour and other factors of production is often an explicit objective of economic integration schemes. Indeed, free mobility of production factors can help to reduce production costs in partner countries where these factors are relatively scarce, attracting productive activity there.

Two empirical examples illustrate this location pattern. Under the colonial period, the economies of Kenya, the United Republic of Tanzania and Uganda were integrated into the East African Community (EAC). Many foreign firms set up during this period were built targeting the regional market. Kenya, with its relatively modern production infrastructure, was used as the industrial hub of the community, which hosted regional branches of multinational corporations wishing to take advantage of the relatively large market. After the collapse of the EAC in 1977, Kenya's export market was substantially reduced and firms established with large installed capacity to serve the regional market were forced to curtail their activities (Mwega and Ndung'u, 2008).[3] In fact, a number of multinational corporations which had subsidiaries in Kenya divested from the country after the collapse of the EAC (Himbara, 1994).

The negative effect of economic de-integration is also illustrated by the case of Burundi, Rwanda and the Eastern part of the Democratic Republic of the Congo, which formed an integrated market under Belgian colonial rule. Bujumbura was the industrial capital of the region at that time. When the three countries gained independence in the early 1960s, they adopted import-substitution policies, instituting tariff and non-tariff barriers. These policies hurt Burundi's export to the Democratic Republic of the Congo and Rwanda as the country lost more than half of its external market. As the market shrank, de-integration led to smaller firm size. Microeconomic survey evidence shows that in 1962–1963, just after independence, Burundian firms' capacity utilization dropped from near full capacity to between 25 per cent and 50 per cent on average. Smaller markets required smaller firm size, so it is not surprising that manufacturing firms created in Burundi before 1960 had a productive capacity 2.4 times larger than those created afterwards (Nkurunziza and Ngaruko, 2008).

It should be noted that, despite the positive effects of regional integration presented above, some criticisms have been aired as well. Proponents of free trade, for example, argue that regional trade blocs limit rather than encourage global trade expansion (Schiff, 1997; World Bank, 2000). They base their argument on the fact that regional blocs tend to raise tariff and non-tariff walls around them, reducing trade flows from outside the bloc. This, as a result, may lead to inefficiencies in resource allocation and production, reducing the welfare gains from competition, as discussed earlier. Therefore, despite the popularity of trade blocs over the last several decades, not all economists share the view that they have a positive net effect on trade. Attempts to empirically measure this effect for specific trade blocs have contributed to shedding light on the ongoing debate (see chapter 2). Some concepts used to measure the effect of regionalism on trade will be discussed in the next chapter.[4]

B. Historical overview of economic integration in Africa

Since the independence era, virtually all African countries have embraced regionalism. Today, there are more regional organizations in Africa than in any other continent and most African countries are engaged in more than one regional integration initiative (see figure 1). Regional integration appeared to be the framework to address obstacles to intra-African trade; reducing barriers to intra-African trade will create larger regional markets that can realize economies of scale and sustain production systems and markets as well as enhance Africa's competitiveness. In the period from the 1960s to the 1980s, over 200 intergovernmental multi-sectoral economic cooperation organizations had been established and over 120 single sectoral multi-national and bilateral organizations (Adedeji, 2002).

The commitment to regionalism was part and parcel of the broader aspiration of continental integration, which takes its roots from the Pan-African movement of shared values, collective self-reliance in development and political independence. From the beginning of the decolonization process in the 1960s, the establishment of subregional economic communities was a significant part of Africa's development strategy.

In the period from the 1960s to the 1980s, several intergovernmental economic cooperation organizations were established to promote technical and economic cooperation. These regional agreements in Africa generally sought to (a) expand the growth of intraregional trade by removing tariffs and non tariffs barriers; (b) strengthen regional development, through the promotion of economic sectors, regional infrastructures and the establishment of large scale manufacturing projects; (c) remove barriers to the free movement of production factors; and (d) promote monetary cooperation. During this period, many African countries implemented highly interventionist and protectionist trade regimes, motivated by several concerns, among which were fiscal concern and the protection of domestic industry, in the context of import-substitution industrialization strategy.

The Lagos Plan of Action (LPA), adopted in April 1980 in response to the deteriorating economic situation in Africa, proposed a strategy for shifting Africa to a sustainable development path which calls for an inversion of the experience since the 1960s. The LPA encourages the pursuit of three goals: (a) high and sustained economic growth; (b) transformation of the economic and social structures; and (c) maintenance of a sustainable resource base. Regional and subregional integration constitutes the principal impulse in restructuring the fragmented African continent into more coherent and stronger economic regional and subregional entities. The overarching objective of the LPA remains the achievement of effective regional integration though national and collective self-reliance. But during this period, African trade policy and general economic development strategy have experienced two contrasting tendencies (Oyejide, 2005). While collectively, African countries have embarked on an inward-looking regional strategy — which implies an inward-oriented import-substitution industrialization strategy based on protected regional markets — during the mid-1980s, African countries at the individual country level started rationalizing and liberalizing their trade regime in the framework of the structural adjustment programmes of the World Bank and the International Monetary Fund, the outward-oriented focus of which implied the closer integration of Africa into the world economy. During this period, the attention of African policymakers shifted from regional integration to the implementation of structural adjustment and economic liberalization programmes. Thus, this period stalled the effective working of many regional groupings in Africa.

Nevertheless, African countries continued to consider the regional approach as the best tool for their development. A new chapter in the history of African regional integration commenced in Abuja, Nigeria, on 3 June 1991. The treaty establishing the AEC committed the continent along the path of economic integration. This treaty calls for the establishment of the AEC by 2027, with a common currency, full mobility of the factors of production, and free movement of goods and services among African countries. The year 2001 saw an acceleration of policy discussions on regional integration with the establishment of the African Union (AU) and the launch of the New Partnership for African Development (NEPAD). NEPAD focuses on the provision of essential regional public goods (such as transport, energy, water, information and communication technology, disease eradication, environmental preservation and provision of regional research capacity), as well as the promotion of intra-African trade and investments. The focus is on rationalizing the institutional framework for economic integration, by identifying common projects compatible with integrated country and regional development programmes, and on the harmonization of economic and investment policies and practices.

There are 14 major regional economic groupings in Africa with varying degrees of integration, as summarized in table 1 below.

Table 1

Major African RECs

Major Regional Economic Communities (RECs)	Type	Areas of integration and co-operation include:	Date of entry into force	Member States	Specified objective
Arab Maghreb Union (UMA)	Free Trade Area	Goods, services, investment, migration	17 Feb. 1989	Algeria, Libyan Arab Jamahiriya, Mauritania, Morocco, Tunisia	Full economic union
Common Market for Eastern and Southern Africa (COMESA)	Free Trade Area	Goods, services, investment, migration	8 Dec. 1994	Angola, Burundi, Comoros, Democratic Republic of the Congo, Djibouti, Egypt, Eritrea, Ethiopia, Kenya, Madagascar, Malawi, Mauritius, Namibia, Rwanda, Seychelles, Sudan, Swaziland, Uganda, Zambia, Zimbabwe	Common market
Community of Sahel-Saharan States (CEN-SAD)	Free Trade Area	Goods, services, investment, migration	4 Feb. 1998	Benin, Burkina Faso, Central African Republic, Chad, Côte d'Ivoire, Djibouti, Egypt, Eritrea, Gambia, Libya, Mali, Morocco, Niger, Nigeria, Senegal, Somalia, Sudan, Togo, Tunisia	Free trade area and integration in some sectors
Economic Community of Central African States (ECCAS)	Free Trade Area	Goods, services, investment, migration	1 July 2007	Angola, Burundi, Cameroon, Central African Republic, Chad, Congo, Democratic Republic of the Congo, Equatorial Guinea, Gabon, Sao Tome and Principe, Rwanda	Full economic union
Economic Community of West African States (ECOWAS)	Free Trade Area	Goods, services, investment, migration	24 July 1993	Benin, Burkina Faso, Cape Verde, Côte d'Ivoire, Gambia, Ghana, Guinea, Guinea-Bissau, Liberia, Mali, Niger, Nigeria, Senegal, Sierra Leone, Togo	Full economic union
Inter-Governmental Authority on Development (IGAD)	Free Trade Area	Goods, services, investment, migration	25 Nov. 1996	Djibouti, Eritrea, Ethiopia, Kenya, Somalia, Sudan, Uganda	Full economic union
Southern African Development Community (SADC)	Free Trade Area	Goods, services, investment, migration	1 Sep. 2000	Angola, Botswana, Democratic Republic of the Congo, Lesotho, Malawi, Mauritius, Mozambique, Namibia, Seychelles, South Africa, Swaziland, United Republic of Tanzania, Zambia, Zimbabwe	Full economic union
Economic and Monetary Community of Central Africa (CEMAC)	Customs Union	Goods, services, investment, migration	24 June 1999	Cameroon, Central African Republic, Chad, Congo, Equatorial Guinea, Gabon	Full economic union
East African Community (EAC)	Customs Union	Goods, services, investment, migration	7 July 2000	Kenya, United Republic of Tanzania, Uganda, Rwanda, Burundi	Full economic union
Southern African Customs Union (SACU)	Customs Union	Goods, services, investment, migration	15 July 2004	Botswana, Lesotho, Namibia, South Africa, Swaziland	Custom union
West African Economic and Monetary Union (UEMOA)	Customs Union	Business law harmonized. Macroeconomic policy convergence in place	10 Jan. 1994	Benin, Burkina Faso, Côte d'Ivoire, Guinea-Bissau, Mali, Niger, Senegal, Togo	Full economic union

Source: UNCTAD secretariat.

The main message from this table is that Africa is deepening its regional integration by integrating non-traditional issues such as services, investment and migration in regional programmes linking African countries.

The AU classifies these groupings into two: RECs and other integration blocs.

One notable characteristic of regional integration in Africa has been the multitude of regional integration initiatives and consequently the participation of African countries in several of these regional trade agreements (RTAs). Many African countries hold multiple memberships. Of the 53 countries, 27 are members of two regional groupings, 18 belong to three, and one country is a member of four. Only seven countries have maintained membership in one bloc. Multiple arrangements and institutions, as well as overlapping membership in the same region, tend to confuse integration goals and lead to counterproductive competition between countries and institutions (ECA, 2008). To overcome this situation, African leaders attempted to achieve more rationalization of regional integration initiatives.

In their search for unity and collective development strategy, African countries have also proposed a number of external partnerships, which the continent has endeavored to cope with collectively. Among these external partnerships are (a) multilateral partnerships in the framework of the World Trade Organization (WTO); (b) the African, Caribbean and Pacific Group of States (ACP)–European Union (EU) partnership, through economic partnerships agreements (EPAs); and (c) a growing number of bilateral initiatives in support of African development, such as the African Growth and Opportunity Act (AGOA, United States), the Tokyo International Conference on African Development (TICAD, Japan), and initiatives from China, India and Brazil. Turkey proposed recently to enter in a partnership with Africa. African countries have been trying to bring such initiatives into a continental framework under the African Union, to bring about greater synergy and ensure a mutually beneficial outcome for partner countries.

There are also regional integration arrangements made up of regional initiatives, which link African countries into North–South trade arrangements. In spite of the growth trends in intra-REC trade, the pattern of REC exports continues to be strongly influenced by historical links with the outside world. In the majority of the RECs, over 80 per cent of exports are still destined for markets outside Africa, with the European Union and the United States accounting for over 50 per cent of this total. Notwithstanding geographical proximity, African countries trade more with the EU than with other economies inside Africa (ECA, 2008).

Figure 1
Africa: Overlapping membership in regional integration groups

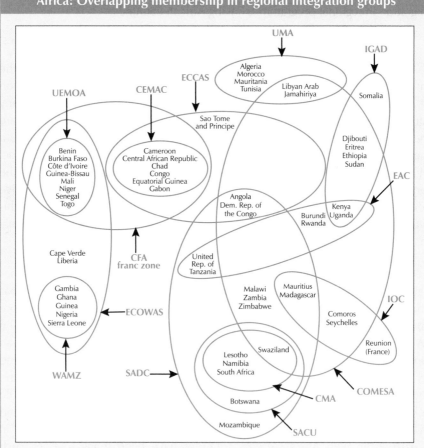

Source: UNCTAD secretariat.

Note: Comoros is also a member of the Communauté financière africaine (CFA) franc zone; The EAC is the regional intergovernmental organization of Kenya, Uganda, the United Republic of Tanzania, Burundi and Rwanda. Rwanda and Burundi acceded to the EAC Treaty on 18 June 2007 and became full members of the community 1 July 2007.

Economic Partnership Agreements (EPAs): The Cotonou Agreement signed on 23 June 2000 in Cotonou, Benin, established a new framework for cooperation over trade and aid between the EU and the 78 members of ACP. It replaced four successive Lomé conventions, the first of which was signed in 1975. It envisaged establishing free trade areas between the EU and each of the regional groupings, the EPAs. For that purpose, the African regional groupings are centered on

COMESA, SADC, CEMAC and ECOWAS. In the framework of the EPAs, unilateral preferences will be replaced by reciprocal free trade arrangements in order to make the EPAs WTO-compatible. They will have a comprehensive coverage of trade and trade-related measures (trade in goods and services, investment, competition, trade facilitation, and Aid for Trade), as provided for by the Cotonou Agreement. A differentiation will be made in the treatment of least developed countries (LDCs) and non-LDCs. Finally, the EPAs have an Aid for Trade component.

South Africa FTA with the EU: The EU and South Africa on 11 October 1999 concluded an agreement on trade, development and cooperation, designed to strengthen cooperation in various fields. This agreement pursues several objectives, including promoting regional cooperation and the country's economic integration in southern Africa and in the world economy, and expanding and liberalizing trade in goods, services and capital between the parties.

Trade, Investment and Development Cooperation Agreement (TIDCA) between SACU and the United States (2008): On 16 July 2008, the TIDCA between the United States and the Southern African Customs Union (SACU) was signed in Washington, D.C. On entering into the negotiations, SACU's main objectives were among others to promote deeper regional integration.

AGOA was signed into law on 18 May 2000, as Title 1 of the Trade and Development Act of 2000. The act offers tangible incentives for African countries to continue their efforts to open their economies and build free markets.

United States Trade and Investment Framework Agreement (TIFA): TIFA is a consultative mechanism for the United States to discuss issues affecting trade and investment with another country. TIFAs have been negotiated predominantly with countries that are in the beginning stages of opening up their economies to international trade and investment, either because they were traditionally isolated or had closed economies. In recent years, the United States has concluded many TIFAs, including with (a) the African countries of Algeria, Tunisia, Nigeria, Ghana and South Africa; and (b) two RECs, UEMOA and COMESA. Although TIFAs are non-binding, they can yield direct benefits by addressing specific trade problems and by helping trading partners develop the experience, institutions and rules that advance integration into the global economy, creating momentum for liberalization that in some cases can lead to a free trade agreement (FTA).[5]

These North–South regional integration agreements are now interacting in complex ways with the African economic integration efforts and adding another layer to the complexity of the spaghetti bowl of regional integration.

C. Brief assessment of the performance of regional integration efforts in Africa

Overall, some regional groupings have made some progress in their attempts to integrate, but the performance is mixed. The following promising cases are to be noted: CEMAC has managed to form a monetary and customs union. It has harmonized the competition and business regulatory framework and there is a move towards macroeconomic convergence. COMESA has designed single rules of origin and has simplified its customs procedures. It has also achieved the elimination of non-tariff barriers (in particular import licensing), the removal of foreign exchange restrictions, and the removal of import and export quotas. SADC has achieved the harmonization of policies in taxation, investment, stock exchange and insurance, while achieving macroeconomic convergence. In other developmental cooperation areas, such as, for example, the power pool, it has likewise made good progress. ECOWAS has removed tariffs on raw materials and has made progress towards macroeconomic policy convergence. A customs union has been established and harmonization of business regulatory framework and convergence on macroeconomic policies has been reached.

Regional initiatives in Africa, however, did not deliver much to uplift the economic conditions of its members nor ensure sustainable growth and liberalization. Intraregional trade as a proportion of total trade remains much lower in African regional integration arrangements compared to those of the Asian and Latin American regions. Some regional groupings in Africa have failed to boost the exports of the areas covered. For example, today CEMAC displays the lowest intraregional trade share of all regional integration schemes in Africa (less than 2 per cent). The benefits from regional integration are not the same for all members of these groupings. In the ECOWAS regions for example, three countries (Nigeria, Côte d'Ivoire and Senegal) account for almost 90 per cent of all intraregional exports and almost 50 per cent of all intraregional imports. Trade liberalization within the regions covered by African regional integration has likewise been generally low.

Other explanations of these failures essentially rely on initial conditions, the problems of implementation, and basic design deficiency. Initial conditions relate, for instance, to the lack of complementarities among regional partners in goods and factors of production, and potentials for product differentiation between regional partners emanating from differences in income levels and consumption patterns. In addition, most African regional integrations were established without strong private sector support, while many of the schemes lacked viable mechanisms for redistributing benefits from the net gainers to the more disadvantaged regional partners. For most of the regional integration schemes, there was almost complete non-implementation of agreed trade liberalization schedules as well as other obligations by members. African regional integration was undertaken by countries whose basic development strategy during the 1960s and 1970s was essentially inward-oriented. The policy environment generated by this strategy contained an inherent anti-export bias. It thus had negative implications for regional integration as the supra-national authority of the regional integration was often explicitly contested or implicitly ignored. This is clearly a design fault. Many regional integration initiatives were over-ambitious; they had overlapping memberships and mandates that sometimes conflicted and were often unclear.

There remain economic and institutional challenges to furthering intraregional trade in Africa. The economic obstacles include the high dependence of most member countries on export of primary commodities, the strict rules of origin emanating from trade liberalization schemes and the poor quality of infrastructure (ECA, 2008).

Institutional challenges include bureaucratic and physical hindrances, such as road charges, transit fees and administrative delays at borders and ports. These hindrances raise transport costs and render deliveries unreliable. Other challenges are related to the lack of coordination and harmonization of policies and regulations at the regional level, non-implementation issues and overlapping membership.

Despite these problems, there is a new optimism that intraregional trade and regional integration can help promote development if past mistakes are remedied (Njinkeu and Powo Fosso, 2006). For African leaders, the imperatives for regional cooperation are stronger now than ever before, given the multiple socio-economic and political impacts of globalization on the African continent. The AU offers the political framework through which Africa would like to be linked before integrating into the rest of the world. The increased emphasis on policy integration and the search for deep integration — including creation of a common market for goods, services, capital and people involving harmonization of rules — are indicative of the recent changes occurring in the regional integration initiatives in Africa. Also, the recent shift in designing and implementing programmes deepen cooperation and integration beyond trade to encompass integration in key sectors and areas where cross-border externalities are significant — such as transportation, energy, telecommunications, finances, monetary and exchange rate, business laws, migration, investment policies and competition (ECA, 2008). This new wave of regionalism aims at reducing risks and transaction costs for private sector activities, and at realizing an open and unified regional economic area (Njinkeu and Powo Fosso, 2006).

This report seeks to provide some insights, which might contribute to the new dynamism of regionalism in Africa.

D. Conclusion

Regional integration has been and remains a top priority for African governments. The various regional economic cooperation initiatives, while moving at different paces in terms of implementation of the provisions of their respective treaties, are showing some progress, even if it is slow. Some of the main challenges relate to the lack of political will on the part of some governments to enforce the necessary reforms in their respective countries, including making the necessary amendments to their laws and regulations, and the workings of their institutions. There are also challenges related to economic preparedness, as members of economic communities are not always as economically proximate as they are geographically. The idea of regionalism has to also be marketed at home, which is easier for some countries than others.

But the imperatives for strengthening regional cooperation are acknowledged both at the regional and at the national levels. Globalization and liberalization have integrated markets elsewhere and made movements of the factors of production easier — developments that have profound economic, political and social implications on the African continent and its citizens. Recognizing the challenges of globalization, African leaders have consistently expressed their desire to deepen regional integration, including through the creation of a common market for goods, services, capital and labour, and the harmonization of rules. There are positive developments in this direction. In the interim, several concrete cooperation initiatives are being undertaken to facilitate trade through the forging regional and subregional cooperation schemes in the area of key infrastructure services such as transportation, tourism, energy and telecommunications, as well as initiatives to better facilitate investment and the movement of people within the community.

Chapter 2

EXPANDING INTRA-AFRICAN TRADE FOR AFRICA'S GROWTH

The discussion in chapter 1 shows that the development of the theory of regionalism has been dominated by trade considerations. Even the concepts used to analyse the economic effects of economic integration, such as trade creation and trade diversion (see below), are trade-centric. Trade, therefore, occupies a special place in the discourse on economic integration. However, theory alone cannot fully predict the pattern of intra-African trade. As in most analyses of trade flows, a careful empirical investigation is needed to understand the level, composition and direction of intra-African trade, as well as its determinants. This is the objective of chapter 2. Indeed, this chapter shows that effective regional integration in Africa can substantially increase intra-African trade, which in turn offers an opportunity for economic growth and development.

An important question in this analysis is: considering that the absolute amounts of the current and past flows are small, what is the potential for increasing intra-African trade flows? The analysis finds that there are important unexploited trade opportunities within Africa. However, realizing this potential will require addressing some key impediments to trade. Prominent among these is poor infrastructure, both soft and physical, as it increases transport costs substantially, which in turn reduces the competitiveness of the traded goods.

The present chapter, which focuses on trade in goods, starts by presenting some basic concepts used to measure the effects of regional economic integration on trade. This is followed by an analysis of the direction and composition of trade flows from Africa, contrasting intra-African trade with Africa's trade with the rest of the world. Then, a relatively detailed discussion of the determinants of intra-African trade is carried out. The chapter concludes with a forward-looking view on the future of intra-African trade in the light of recent major developments in the world economy.

A. Trade gains from RTAs

Two questions are discussed in this section: (a) What are the concepts used to assess the gains from regional economic integration? (b) What is the tool available to predict intra-African trade and its determinants?

1. Basic concepts

The basic concepts used to estimate trade gains from regionalism have been discussed in the context of customs union theory. Viner (1950) laid the foundations of this theory by showing that regionalism could result in "trade creation" and "trade diversion". Following the creation of a trade bloc, the removal of trade barriers creates a large market where the low-cost country producing consumer goods increases its market share by capturing the integrated market for the cheaply produced good. This could allow the low-cost producer to further lower production costs thanks to scale economies, availability of more suppliers and specialization effects (Corden, 1972). The movement of demand from the high-cost country to the low-cost country creates new trade for the low-cost country, resulting in "trade creation".

Trade diversion occurs when a partner country's production displaces lower-cost imports from outside the RTA thanks to the high level of protection enjoyed by producers within the RTA. Obviously, the level of protection erected against outside competition is a key determinant of the extent of trade dispersion. If the external tariff is set in such a way that a more expensive internal source of an input or a consumer good replaces the cheaper source from outside the RTA, consumers are penalized because they pay higher prices after integration. That is referred to as "trade diversion".

The overall effect of regionalism on trade in Africa could be positive or negative, depending on which of the two effects dominates. The net gain for the countries involved is positive when the effect of trade creation outweighs that of trade diversion. Indeed, a successful integration process is one which allows trade creation to take place without imposing excessive external tariffs. Otherwise, high external tariffs can protect inefficient firms from competition, a situation that penalizes consumers within the union. Whether regionalism in Africa has led to net trade creation cannot be taken for granted; it is an empirical question.

2. Identifying trade gains from RTAs in Africa

The gravity model is the most popular method used to empirically predict the level of bilateral trade flows between economies and estimate the extent of trade creation and trade diversion.[6] The model is a mathematical equation relating trade between two economies to the key determinants. The latter are grouped into "attraction" and "opposing" forces. For a given country, there are forces that attract trade and others with an opposite effect. The main reason why intra-African trade flows remain low is that the attraction factors are very weak, whereas the opposing forces are very strong. Among the latter, poor soft and hard infrastructure is identified as the main impediment to increasing intra-African trade (see section 3 for details).

Some authors have noted that, due to trade diversion, the economic benefits of regional trading arrangements in developing regions, and Africa in particular, are doubtful (Schiff, 1997; World Bank, 2000).[7] Others have argued that economic integration is what Africa needs to address its problem of fragmented national economies (Elbadawi, 1997). Empirical results are also mixed. For example, using a gravity model, a study covering 41 sub-Saharan African countries in the period 1988–1997 found no evidence of trade creation or trade diversion effects, suggesting that overall, trading blocs in Africa have not been able to positively affect the flows of trade in a significant way (Longo and Sekkat, 2004).[8]

In contrast, several studies specifically documenting the effect of regional trading arrangements in developing regions uncovered unambiguous evidence of trade creation. For example, evidence for trade creation was found for the three main African trade blocs, namely COMESA, ECOWAS and SADC (Cernat, 2001). There is also empirical evidence that the overall effect of economic integration on trade creation within CEMAC is positive (Gbetnkom, 2008).

The fact that some studies have not found econometric evidence for trade creation following regional integration should not be interpreted as meaning that regionalism in Africa can not have a positive affect on the flow of trade. The lack of evidence could be due to several factors, including heterogeneity of the samples used in the estimation, a serious problem that has been overlooked in many studies (Fontagné et al., 2002). This could be the reason why studies using more homogeneous regional samples to analyze trade flows among countries in a specific trading group tend to find a positive effect whereas global studies, which are more heterogeneous, fail to find such an effect (Cernat, 2001; Gbetnkom, 2008; Longo and Sekkat, 2004). Moreover, the lack of evidence for a positive effect of integration on intra-African trade could be due to the presence of too many obstacles to trade in comparison with other regions. For example, institutional factors such as poor economic policy and internal political tensions in Africa seem to keep regional trade at a very low level (Longo and Sekkat, 2004). The implication is that an improvement in these negative factors would increase the positive effect of regionalism on trade flows.

As discussed in chapter 1, the question is not whether Africa should integrate or not; there is a political consensus for regional integration in Africa. The issue is how to maximize the benefits of integration, including trade flows. If regional integration can increase intra-African trade under some conditions, the issue is how to identify these conditions and determine how they could be satisfied. For example, why is intra-African trade in Africa only a fraction of the level in other developing countries (table 2)? What should Africa do to reach a level of intraregional trade comparable to that in other developing regions? Responding to these questions requires information on the main determinants of intra-African trade and the ways in which they can be modified in such a way that they increase trade flows. Empirical data in sections 2 and 3 show that regional integration could have an important growth effect on trade if some key constraints were properly addressed.

B. Trends and patterns of Africa's merchandise trade flows

1. Global picture

Despite the long history of regional integration on the continent, the level of intra-African trade remains low in comparison with intraregional trade in other regions, both developed and developing. Over the period 2004–2006, intra-African exports represented 8.7 per cent of the region's total exports. Intra-African imports, on the other hand, represented 9.6 per cent of total imports. This proportion was substantially higher for sub-Saharan Africa (around 12 per cent) than for North Africa (around 3 per cent).[9] Nonetheless, even the sub-Saharan African proportion of intraregional trade remains far below other regions', as can be seen in table 2.

Table 2
  Intraregional imports and exports as a proportion of total trade,
                    2004–2006 averages
                        (Per cent)

	Imports	Exports
Africa	9.6	8.7
Developing America	20.9	18.5
Developing Asia	48.1	45.5
Developed America	23.3	39.8
Developed Europe	68.1	71.4
Source: UNCTAD, 2008c.		

The current situation as summarized in table 2 is not a recent phenomenon. Looking back over the period 1960–2006, it appears that Africa has consistently had a considerably lower proportion of intraregional trade than other regions. Indeed, it is the only region in which the proportion of intraregional exports was lower than 10 per cent in 1960. This was largely a consequence of the pattern of trade favoured by colonial rulers, which was extractive and outward-oriented, and did not encourage African countries to develop strong trade linkages among themselves. While developing America's share of intraregional exports fluctuated around its 1960 level, other regions – most notably developing Asia – experienced marked increases in their intraregional trade (see figure 2). In Asia, regional integration has largely occurred as a result of the pattern of economic growth in the region which took place within a context of fairly weak regional institutions (UNCTAD, 2007c).

Though the proportion of Africa's intraregional trade remains low in comparison, it has increased considerably over the years, albeit from a very low level. This proportion has gone through several distinct phases. It was initially stable through to the early 1970s before plunging during that decade to a low point reached in 1978, with intra-African exports worth only 2.9 per cent of total African exports. From there, it recovered slowly until the mid-1980s, then increased sharply in the second half of the 1980s and the first half of the 1990s.

Several events during the same period could explain the increase. The low initial level could be explained by the fact that at independence, African countries inherited trade links which were almost exclusively oriented towards Europe. The reason was that African colonies were used to produce commodities feeding colonial powers' industries. This pattern also reflected the continent's relative endowment in natural resources, particularly at a time when Africa's industrial

Figure 2
Intraregional exports as a proportion of total exports, 1960–2006

Legend: Africa — Developing America — Developing Asia — Developed America — Developed Europe

Source: UNCTAD, 2008c.

sector was rudimentary. This did not particularly encourage trade with other African countries, which explains the very low level on intra-African trade in the 1960s and 1970s. To some extent, African trade is still influenced by this colonial legacy. Moreover, the import-substitution policies pursued in the 1960s and 1970s were not encouraging trade among African countries. They were centred on self-sufficiency but had difficulty achieving this objective, as illustrated by widespread rationing in several countries, particularly in the late 1970s and early 1980s.

The positive trend starting in the early 1980s can be explained by three important events. First, the adoption of structural adjustment programmes in many countries opened up African economies, creating a new environment following the import-substitution era. More trade opportunities among African countries were created, even if African countries were unable to fully benefit from this environment, (UNCTAD, 2008a). The second event was the end of apartheid in South Africa and subsequent deepening of economic ties with its neighbours (Metzger, 2008). The third event was the intensification of RTAs with the foundation of UMA in 1989, SADC in 1992, and COMESA in 1994.

Since the early 2000s, the proportion of intra-African merchandise trade has stabilized at about 10 per cent, with a slight decline towards the end of the period. This does not, however, mean that the absolute value of intra-African trade has stagnated or declined. The stagnation of the proportion is due to the fact that Africa's trade with the rest of the world increased much faster than intra-African trade. Indeed, whereas intra-African trade increased by 13.64 per cent per year, on average, between 1999 and 2006, the average yearly increases in Africa's trade with the United States was 27.57 per cent, while trade with China increased at a yearly rate of 60.85 per cent over the same period. Therefore, the stagnation of the rate of intra-African trade is mainly due to the growing importance of Africa's new trade partners.

Overall, taking the increase from the levels seen in the first three years of the 1960s to the level of 2004–2006, the increase is greater in Africa than in all other regions except developing Asia. Within Africa, North Africa has systematically had a much lower proportion of intraregional trade than sub-Saharan Africa, which is surprising given the linguistic and cultural similarities among North African countries. Sub-Saharan Africa, in contrast, has had an impressive record of growth of its intraregional exports. Table 3 shows that, relative to other regions, sub-Saharan Africa has had a considerably higher rate of growth in its intraregional exports share over the period 1960–1962 to 2004–2006.

Table 3
Intraregional exports as a percentage of total exports, 1960–1962 and 2004–2006

	1960–1962	2004–2006	Growth (in %)
Africa	5.58	8.68	55.43
North Africa	2.81	2.45	-12.75
Sub-Saharan Africa	4.08	11.41	179.94
Developing America	15.97	18.54	16.11
Developing Asia	21.06	45.54	116.28
Developed America	26.64	39.80	49.41
Developed Europe	61.28	71.38	16.47

Source: UNCTAD, 2008c.

2. African trade destinations: Africa and the rest of the world

From the discussion so far, it is clear that, overall and in comparative terms, intra-African trade does not represent a large proportion of total African trade. However, this aggregate picture hides important country variations. A more precise image of the importance of intra-African trade to specific African countries is provided in table 4, which looks at trade destinations at a country level.

The first message that stands out from table 4 is that, for most countries in the region, intra-African trade is considerably more important than the aggregate figures suggest. Indeed, a simple average of the share of intra-African trade in African countries' exports reveals that it is worth 21 per cent of total exports, a figure that is over twice as large as the aggregate figure for Africa. This also makes Africa by far the second most important export market for most African countries behind Europe. Of the 52 countries in the table, 7 count Africa as their main export market and 25 count it as their second most important export market. The reason for the discrepancy between this finding and the low aggregate figure is simple. Many of the big exporters in Africa trade little with other African countries. This is notably the case with oil-exporting countries such as Algeria, Angola, the Libyan Arab Jamahiriya and Congo.

There are also many countries in the region that depend on intra-African trade to a much greater extent. Five African countries have exports to Africa that are larger than half of their total exports, while a further 14 countries export more than a quarter of their exports to Africa.[10] So, contrary to what the aggregate figure suggests, Africa represents a significant export market for many African countries.

It is also important to note that over three quarters of intra-African trade takes place within regional trading blocs. This suggests that these RTAs represent relevant institutions that should be used as stepping stones for deeper intra-African trade.

3. Exporters and importers

Analysing more closely the trade patterns of the main exporters and importers from the region gives a better understanding of which are the most influential countries and, eventually, where the major trade poles are located. Overall, the list of top exporters to the rest of the world is strongly reflective of the importance of oil in Africa's exports. Indeed, of the 10 top exporters to the rest of the world,

Table 4

African countries' export destinations, 2004–2006

(Per cent)

Country	Developed Europe	United States	Eastern, Southern, and South-Eastern Asia	Western Asia	Africa	To main regional grouping	Name of main regional grouping
Swaziland	1.23	5.54	1.33	0.15	84.83	81.52	SADC
Djibouti	4.16	0.87	3.58	10.47	80.35	32.63	COMESA
Togo	15.71	0.47	13.83	0.20	61.48	57.49	ECOWAS
Mali	21.18	0.23	16.92	0.70	60.29	9.79	ECOWAS
Zimbabwe	23.05	2.87	9.32	1.53	54.53	53.18	SADC
Kenya	26.98	5.66	10.36	3.08	47.36	32.92	COMESA
Senegal	26.34	0.60	12.46	0.80	44.99	37.32	ECOWAS
Malawi	41.15	10.14	3.49	1.13	36.37	28.11	SADC
Namibia	44.75	5.72	5.31	0.69	36.18	35.63	SADC
Uganda	38.72	1.89	6.64	12.81	34.00	29.22	COMESA
Zambia	46.64	0.48	15.75	2.45	33.95	30.66	SADC
Burkina Faso	11.21	0.28	48.73	0.70	33.20	31.37	ECOWAS
Niger	50.93	2.06	0.56	0.12	32.27	30.24	ECOWAS
Rwanda	50.21	2.23	12.41	0.64	31.33	29.63	COMESA
Cape Verde	60.66	4.04	0.10	2.40	29.94	25.34	ECOWAS
Côte d'Ivoire	48.48	11.07	4.99	0.76	28.95	23.62	ECOWAS
Benin	12.45	0.05	56.62	1.82	28.03	21.83	ECOWAS
Ghana	40.79	18.66	7.05	1.95	26.80	9.90	ECOWAS
United Rep. of Tanzania	44.94	1.15	16.79	3.55	26.71	17.78	SADC
Gambia	71.84	0.90	1.57	0.09	24.98	23.81	ECOWAS
Eritrea	36.21	1.25	29.87	4.97	22.19	20.90	COMESA
Lesotho	10.13	70.50	0.04	0.01	18.51	18.38	SADC
Mozambique	48.77	0.98	4.70	0.42	18.11	17.84	SADC
Guinea-Bissau	3.64	7.09	71.39	0.00	17.72	17.65	ECOWAS
Ethiopia	40.27	5.04	12.16	14.23	15.37	9.31	COMESA
South Africa	38.98	11.20	13.50	2.47	14.87	10.15	SADC
Burundi	65.21	0.19	1.22	17.96	13.64	12.29	COMESA
Botswana	83.16	1.91	0.24	0.04	13.41	13.36	SADC
Cameroon	66.50	5.66	6.57	1.10	12.26	5.71	ECCAS
Central African Republic	75.36	0.18	2.15	1.18	11.26	10.61	ECCAS
Mauritius	66.56	10.81	3.42	7.70	9.03	7.38	SADC
Nigeria	23.37	47.79	6.91	0.52	8.78	5.26	ECOWAS
Tunisia	71.86	0.66	2.63	2.03	8.64	7.06	UMA
Dem. Rep. of the Congo	52.19	10.87	14.90	0.04	6.42	5.32	COMESA
Sao Tome and Principe	88.56	0.00	0.01	0.00	6.23	4.81	ECCAS
Mauritania	60.82	0.01	2.72	0.17	6.17	3.35	UMA
Egypt	35.33	8.49	13.05	16.44	5.90	3.45	COMESA
Gabon	16.62	59.48	14.35	0.20	5.11	1.35	ECCAS
Liberia	70.71	7.56	13.74	0.89	4.99	0.59	ECOWAS
Madagascar	54.47	23.04	8.46	1.27	4.66	3.26	COMESA
Morocco	75.23	2.72	6.90	2.52	4.46	1.49	UMA
Somalia	1.42	0.28	17.06	76.68	3.87	..	
Sierra Leone	55.85	10.06	2.60	0.47	2.35	1.52	ECOWAS
Libyan Arab Jamahiriya	80.45	4.89	3.50	7.09	2.25	1.86	UMA
Guinea	50.83	8.33	11.47	0.05	2.25	1.31	ECOWAS
Algeria	54.44	24.89	2.73	3.94	2.18	1.01	UMA
Sudan	3.69	0.15	76.51	9.04	2.00	1.69	COMESA
Congo	6.88	31.61	56.33	0.36	1.70	0.60	ECCAS
Angola	11.01	39.10	39.71	0.05	1.59	1.53	SADC
Seychelles	60.32	0.32	1.36	36.56	0.87	0.19	COMESA
Equatorial Guinea	28.26	26.10	34.21	0.22	0.26	0.03	ECCAS
Chad	9.68	73.14	16.69	0.01	0.20	0.01	ECCAS

Source: UNCTAD, 2008c.

Note: Countries are ranked by descending order according to the proportion of their exports going to other African countries.

Box 1. Trade within RTAs

COMESA: The main exporter is Kenya, with over a third of total regional exports, followed distantly by Zambia and Egypt. Average value of total exports over 2004–2006 was just under $3 billion. Over that period, intra-group exports represented 5 per cent of total group exports. The main importers are Uganda, Sudan, the Democratic Republic of the Congo and Egypt, but overall the shares of imports are more balanced. The main linkages that emerge are Kenyan exports to Uganda, which alone are responsible for 17 per cent of all intra-COMESA exports. Egypt's exports are mainly to its neighbours Sudan and the Libyan Arab Jamahiriya, with Kenya a distant third. Zambia has strong exports to the Democratic Republic of the Congo, Zimbabwe, Egypt and Malawi.

EAC: The average value of exports within the EAC between 2004 and 2006 was around $1.2 billion per annum. That represented 20 per cent of total group exports. The main exporter is Kenya, which accounts for nearly three quarters of intra-group exports, while Uganda's exports are 12 per cent of the group total. Imports are better balanced, with Uganda absorbing 44 per cent of intra-group imports followed by the United Republic of Tanzania (22 per cent) and Kenya (17 per cent). The relations that really stand out are Kenyan exports to Uganda, which alone account for 42 per cent of total intra-group trade, as well as Kenya's exports to the United Republic of Tanzania, which are worth 21 per cent of group trade. It should be noted that, despite their small size, Burundi and Rwanda have a substantial impact on intra-group trade, as they respectively absorb 6 and 11 per cent of intra-group imports. Also, even though these two countries' impact on the total value of intra-group exports is low, exports to the group are important to both countries. Indeed, intra-group exports represent over 11 per cent of Burundi's total and over a quarter of Rwanda's.

ECCAS: The average value of intra-group exports between 2004 and 2006 was the lowest of all considered RTAs. Only $320 million of exports were traded, which is under 1 per cent of total group exports. The main exporter is Cameroon, with over half of total intra-group exports, followed by Gabon (19 per cent) and Congo (13 per cent). Imports are better balanced, with main importers being the Democratic Republic of the Congo (22 per cent), Gabon, Congo and Chad. The most important linkages in value terms are exports from Cameroon to the Democratic Republic of the Congo, Gabon, Congo and Chad.

ECOWAS: The annual average value of intra-group exports between 2004 and 2006 was $5.4 billion, which represented around 9.4 per cent of ECOWAS' total exports. The main exporters within the group are Nigeria and Côte d'Ivoire, which together account for over 70 per cent of total intra-group exports, followed by Senegal with just under 10 per cent. The major importers are Côte d'Ivoire, Ghana and Nigeria. The main trade linkage is bilateral trade between Nigeria and Côte d'Ivoire, as well as Nigerian exports to Ghana. Also notable are exports from Senegal to Mali and from Côte d'Ivoire to Burkina Faso.

SADC: The average value of intra-group exports between 2004 and 2006 was just under $11 billion per annum. This was equivalent to about 12 per cent of the group's total exports. Unsurprisingly, intra-group imports and exports are dominated by South Africa, which alone represents 44 per cent of intra-group exports and 40 per cent of intra-group imports. The second largest intra-group exporter is Swaziland (14 per cent) and the second largest intra-group importer is Zimbabwe (13 per cent). The most important linkage within the group consists of Swaziland's exports to South Africa, closely followed by South Africa's exports to Zimbabwe, Zambia and Mozambique.

Box 1 (contd.)

UMA: Yearly average intra-group exports between 2004 and 2006 were $ 1.8 billion, which is only 2 per cent of the group's total exports. The main exporter is Tunisia (41 per cent) followed by Algeria and the Libyan Arab Jamahiriya (25 and 23 per cent, respectively). The main importer is Tunisia (31 per cent) followed by the Libyan Arab Jamahiriya and Morocco (28 and 25 per cent, respectively). The main linkages are bilateral trade between Tunisia and the Libyan Arab Jamahiriya, and Algerian exports to Morocco.

Source: UNCTAD, 2008c.

7 are oil and/or gas exporters. Notable exceptions are the relatively diversified economies of South Africa, Morocco and Tunisia (see table 5). As oil is mostly purchased by countries outside the region, the proportion of intra-African trade for many of the large oil-producing countries tends to be low. This is why in 2004–2006, the proportion of intraregional exports without fuels increases to 17 per cent for Africa and 19 per cent for sub-Saharan Africa.[11] Additionally, as a few countries are responsible for most of Africa's exports to the rest of the world, their influence on the region's trade patterns is considerable. Altogether, four countries (of which three are oil producers) account for over half of Africa's total exports to the rest of the world and eight countries together account for over three quarters of it.

The list of top intra-African exporters is noticeably different from that of the top exporters to the rest of the world. Indeed, of 10 countries on each list, only 5 are present on both lists and only three of the 10 top intra-African exporters are oil-producing countries. Two countries are particularly important to intra-African trade. South Africa's exports to the region alone represent almost a quarter of the total, while Nigeria's are worth roughly half that proportion. Overall, there are only five countries whose exports to the region are worth over 5 per cent of the total and these five countries together account for over half of that total (see table 5). It is also clear that, with the exception of central Africa, all regions of the continent are on this list.

Looking at the top importers of African products reveals the vibrant trade in Southern Africa and the large proportion that this represents in the continent's total intra-imports. Of the top 10 importers of African products in Africa, 7 are in southern Africa. This is an indication of the opportunities small and large countries can derive from a strongly integrated economy, particularly in the presence of a strong trade engine such as South Africa. Indeed, this region of Africa is probably the most obvious example of a possible development pole in Africa.

Table 5

Top 10 exporters to Africa and the rest of the world, 2004–2006

Exports to Africa		Exports to the rest of the world	
Country	Share of total intraregional exports	Country	Share of total African exports to the rest of the world
South Africa	24.29	Algeria	17.36
Nigeria	12.37	South Africa	15.98
Côte d'Ivoire	7.40	Nigeria	14.78
Kenya	5.36	Angola	8.80
Swaziland	5.34	Libyan Arab Jamahiriya	8.75
Namibia	3.47	Morocco	4.30
Ghana	3.42	Egypt	4.07
Algeria	3.36	Tunisia	3.87
Tunisia	3.18	Congo	2.36
Zimbabwe	3.04	Côte d'Ivoire	2.09

Source: UNCTAD, 2008c.

It is also interesting to note that 5 of the top 10 importers from within Africa are landlocked countries (see table 6), suggesting that landlocked countries could use their geographical isolation from world markets to develop regional ties that could deepen intra-African trade. The list of the top importers from the rest of the world mainly reflects the relative size of the economies with South Africa accounting for over a quarter of the total and North African countries making up most of the top-ten list along with Nigeria (see table 6).

Table 6

Top 10 importers from Africa and the rest of the world, 2004–2006

Imports from Africa		Imports from the rest of the world	
Country	Share of total	Country	Share of total
South Africa	9.80	South Africa	25.40
Botswana	8.23	Morocco	9.22
Namibia	6.59	Algeria	9.18
Côte d'Ivoire	4.91	Egypt	8.00
Swaziland	4.70	Nigeria	7.73
Zambia	4.58	Tunisia	6.00
Zimbabwe	4.53	Libyan Arab Jamahiriya	3.49
Lesotho	3.45	Sudan	2.92
Nigeria	3.45	Liberia	2.78
Dem. Rep. of the Congo	3.24	Ghana	2.42

Source: UNCTAD, 2008c.

4. Intra-African trade composition

The previous section illustrated the importance that a strategic product such as oil can have on explaining the trade pattern of an entire region. This suggests that the types of products that are traded could be important in explaining the particularities of intra-African trade and how these differ from Africa's trade with the rest of the world.

In terms of exports, the composition of intra-African exports is fairly evenly distributed between fuels, non-fuel primary products and manufactured goods. Non-fuel primary exports represent 30 per cent of the total, 11 per cent of which represents exports of ores and minerals. Hence, agricultural product exports account for only 19 per cent of total intra-African exports, despite the fact that agriculture accounts for nearly 30 per cent of the production of goods in Africa. This is in contrast to manufacturing, which accounts for 21 per cent of the production of goods but 40 per cent of exports. Clearly, agricultural goods are much less trade-intensive within the region than are manufactured goods. This may be due to the fact that there is greater complementarity between manufactured sectors than there is between agricultural sectors across countries. Furthermore, if intra-African trade composition should reflect the relative importance of different economic sectors, another interpretation of this result is that the potential for increasing intra-African trade in agricultural goods remains largely untapped. One implication is that encouraging investment in agro-industries could generate important benefits for African economies (see chapter 4).

Africa's exports to the rest of the world are less balanced between product groups. Sixty per cent of the value of exports was accounted for by fuel exports only. The relative weights of non-fuel primary products excluding ores and minerals, and manufactured goods are half as important as in intra-African trade. The proportion of minerals and ores is almost unchanged (figure 3). Both agricultural and manufactured goods appear as less trade-intensive given that their export proportions are below the proportions of agriculture and manufacturing sectors in Africa.

Similarly, the composition of imports from the rest of the world is more concentrated than that of intra-African imports. For example, manufactured goods account for nearly three quarters of total African imports from the rest of the world, while they represent less than half of the total value of intra-African

Figure 3
Africa's exports to Africa and to the rest of the world, 2004–2006 averages

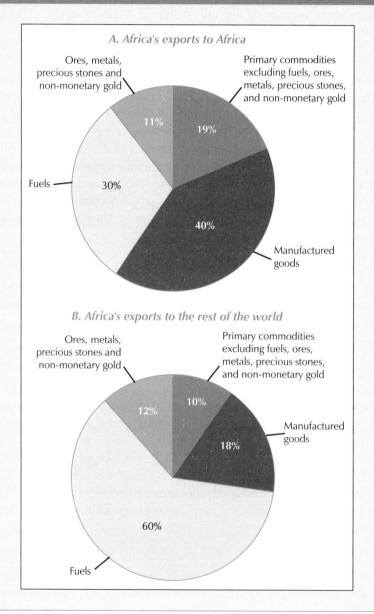

A. *Africa's exports to Africa*

Ores, metals, precious stones and non-monetary gold

Primary commodities excluding fuels, ores, metals, precious stones, and non-monetary gold

11%

19%

Fuels — 30%

40%

Manufactured goods

B. *Africa's exports to the rest of the world*

Ores, metals, precious stones and non-monetary gold

Primary commodities excluding fuels, ores, metals, precious stones, and non-monetary gold

10%

12%

Manufactured goods

18%

60%

Fuels

Source: UNCTAD, 2008c.

imports. Conversely, African imports of fuels and minerals are considerably less important in proportion of the value of imports from the rest of the world than they are for intra-African exports (figure 4).

A more detailed look at the products traded with the rest of the world shows a high concentration of trade around a few products. The top seven exports by value make up more than two thirds of the total.[12] Crude oil alone accounts for nearly 46 per cent of the total. Intra-African trade is less concentrated. Thirty-nine products account for two thirds of intra-African exports. While crude oil is still the most important export product by value, it only accounts for slightly less than 15 per cent of the total.

Overall, the more diversified nature of intra-African trade, when compared with its exports to the rest of the world, suggests that expanding intra-African

Figure 4
African imports from the rest of the world, 2004–2006 averages

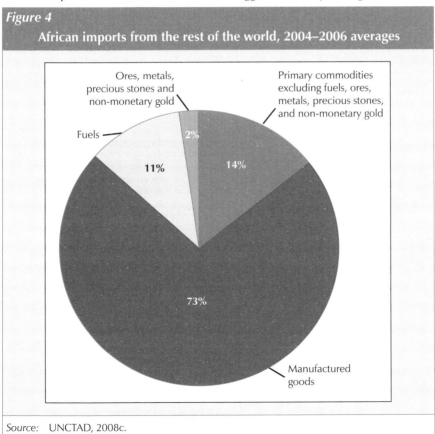

Source: UNCTAD, 2008c.

trade could yield significant benefits to African countries in terms of diversifying their production to non-traditional products and especially manufactures. A closer look at the data reveals that, for 80 per cent of African countries, manufactured products represent a larger share of exports to Africa than they do in total exports.

Combining information on trade composition and the geographical distribution of intra-African trade reveals a number of facts worth noting. First, 18 of the top 25 bilateral trade relations occur within the 6 RTAs listed in box 1, and 10 such relations occur between neighbouring countries (table 7). This

Table 7
Main 25 bilateral intra-African trade relations by value and top 3 products
2004–2006 averages
($ thousands)

Exporter	Importer	Average value 2004–2006	Top 3 exports (% of total)
Swaziland	South Africa	1 319 635	Essential oils, perfume and flavour materials (45%), Sugar, molasses and honey (11%) Articles of apparel, of textile fabrics, n.e.s. (5%)
South Africa	Zimbabwe	1 056 705	Petroleum oils or bituminous minerals > 70 % oil (17%) Maize (not including sweet corn), unmilled (8%) Fertilizers (other than those of group 272) (4%)
Nigeria	Côte d'Ivoire	1 016 878	Petroleum oils, oils from bitumin. materials, crude (>99%) Insectides and similar products, for retail sale (<1%) Cotton fabrics, woven (<1%)
South Africa	Zambia	916 256	Petroleum oils, oils from bitumin. materials, crude (7%) Motor vehic. for transport of goods, special purpose (5%) Fertilizers (other than those of group 272) (4%)
South Africa	Mozambique	900 184	Petroleum oils or bituminous minerals > 70 % oil (19%) Coal, whether or not pulverized, not agglomerated (5%) Sugar, molasses and honey (3%)
Nigeria	South Africa	858 912	Petroleum oils, oils from bitumin. materials, crude (>99%) Non-ferrous base metal waste and scrap, n.e.s. (<1%) Natural rubber and similar gums, in primary forms (<1%)
Nigeria	Ghana	770 166	Petroleum oils, oils from bitumin. materials, crude (98%) Glassware (<1%); Aluminium (<1%)
Namibia	South Africa	695 949	Printed matter (24%) Live animals other than animals of division 03 (11%) Meat of bovine animals, fresh, chilled or frozen (10%)
Ghana	South Africa	604 508	Gold, non-monetary (excluding gold ores and concentrates) (99%) Veneers, plywood, and other wood, worked, n.e.s. (<1%) Wood simply worked, and railway sleepers of wood (<1%)
Mali	South Africa	587 875	Gold, non-monetary (excluding gold ores and concentrates) (>99%); Cotton (<1%) Aircraft and associated equipment; spacecraft, etc. (<1%)

Table 7 (contd.)

Exporter	Importer	Average value 2004–2006	Top 3 exports (% of total)
South Africa	Angola	574 086	Aircraft and associated equipment; spacecraft, etc. (7%) Metal containers for storage or transport (6%) Alcoholic beverages (4%)
Côte d'Ivoire	Nigeria	554 257	Petroleum oils or bituminous minerals > 70 % oil (87%) Perfumery, cosmetics or toilet prepar. (excluding soaps) (5%) Residual petroleum products, n.e.s., related mater. (4%)
Nigeria	Cameroon	530 340	Petroleum oils, oils from bitumin. materials, crude (98%) Ships, boats and floating structures (1%) Rubber tyres, tyre treads or flaps and inner tubes (<1%)
South Africa	Nigeria	523 640	Petroleum oils or bituminous minerals > 70 % oil (16%) Structures and parts, n.e.s., of iron, steel, aluminium (11%) Aluminium (7%)
Zimbabwe	South Africa	502 772	Nickel ores and concentrates; nickel mattes, etc. (30%) Gold, non-monetary (excluding gold ores and concentrates) (18%); Printed matter (11%)
Kenya	Uganda	496 628	Petroleum oils or bituminous minerals > 70 % oil (37%) Lime, cement, fabrica. constr. mat. (excluding glass, clay) (6%); Chocolate, food preparations with cocoa, n.e.s. (4%)
Algeria	Egypt	485 295	Liquefied propane and butane (95%) Natural gas, whether or not liquefied (2%) Petroleum oils or bituminous minerals > 70 % oil (2%)
Tunisia	Libyan Arab Jamahiriya	462 654	Paper and paperboard, cut to shape or size, articles (7%) Fixed vegetable fats and oils, crude, refined, fractio. (6%) Cereal preparations, flour of fruits or vegetables (5%)
South Africa	Kenya	461 999	Flat-rolled prod., iron, non-alloy steel, not coated (26%) Aluminium (5%); Paper and paperboard (4%)
South Africa	United Republic of Tanzania	388 382	Flat-rolled prod., iron, non-alloy steel, not coated (11%) Petroleum oils or bituminous minerals > 70 % oil (9%) Structures and parts, n.e.s., of iron, steel, aluminium (5%)
Zambia	South Africa	379 073	Copper (49%) Copper ores and concentrates; copper mattes, cemen (13%); Cotton (13%)
Libyan Arab Jamahiriya	Tunisia	365 700	Petroleum oils, oils from bitumin. materials, crude (80%) Petroleum gases, other gaseous hydrocarbons, n.e.s. (7%) Iron and steel bars, rods, angles, shapes and sections (3%)
Angola	South Africa	337 912	Petroleum oils, oils from bitumin. materials, crude (>99%) Civil ingineering and contractors' plant and equipment (<1%); Pearls, precious and semi-precious stones (<1%)
Botswana	South Africa	334 825	Meat of bovine animals, fresh, chilled or frozen (7%) Gold, non-monetary (excluding gold ores and concentrates) (6%); Articles of apparel, of textile fabrics, n.e.s. (6%)
Algeria	Morocco	304 797	Liquefied propane and butane (72%) Inorganic chemical elements oxides and halogen salts (10%) Flat-rolled prod. iron non-alloy steel not coated (7%)

Source: UNCTAD, 2008c.
Notes: Products are listed at the SITC three-digit level; n.e.s. means not elsewhere specified.

suggests that, to some degree, the success of African countries is tied to that of their neighbours. Having a prosperous neighbour can positively affect a country's exports. The neighbourhood effect is particularly strong for landlocked countries for reasons discussed in the next section.[13]

Second, the prominence of South Africa in intra-African trade is very clear, as the country participates in 16 of the 25 top trade relations within the continent. More generally, there is a clustering of these relations in Southern Africa. Third, there is also intensive trade among the large coastal economies of Western Africa, and among some of the North African countries. Fourth, Central Africa and the Sahel region are noticeably absent from table 7. This can partially be explained by the fairly small economic size of many of these countries, Sudan being an exception. The answer is also partly found in the poor quality of transport infrastructure in these regions (Buys et al., 2006, and discussion below).

Of the 25 top intra-African trade relations by value, which together account for over half of total intra-African exports, 11 are strongly concentrated on one single product. For seven of these it is petroleum while gold and gas make up the four others. The 14 other trade relations in the list are made up of a more varied list of products. Seven are export flows from South Africa, and five are from other Southern African countries to South Africa. This suggests that intra-African trade, though it is more diversified in terms of products traded than Africa's trade with the rest of the world, remains highly concentrated, not only in geographical terms, but also with respect to a few strategic commodities.

Removing some of the obstacles that impede the expansion of intra-African trade can be expected to change this situation by both making it easier to trade with countries that are at present difficult to reach, especially landlocked countries, and also to make it more economically viable to transport lower value commodities within the region. These obstacles, which are discussed in the next section, include (a) the small size of most African economies; (b) low per capita income, which is a proxy for the level of demand; (c) high trade costs resulting from high transport costs due to poor physical and non-physical infrastructure, including inefficient border procedures; and (d) other trade facilitations mechanisms. Institutional factors such as corruption, poor economic policy and political tensions have a negative effect on the flow of intra-African trade.

C. Explaining the level of intra-African trade

As shown in the previous section, aggregate figures show that intra-African trade is low in comparison to trade within other regions. Some argue that this is to be expected given the low incomes and similar production structures of most African countries. Almost 20 years ago, Foroutan and Pritchett (1993) were among the first economists to investigate whether intra-African trade was too little relative to expectations (they agreed it was too little in absolute terms). Their conclusion was that the level of intra-African trade was not below expectation.

Although this finding has been used in subsequent debates on intra-African trade, it needs to be taken with caution for the following reasons. First, the data used in the paper, covering only 19 African countries, is 20 years old now so it may not reflect the current realities. Second, the sample excluded South Africa, which is by far the most important intra-African trade actor, as shown in the previous section. It is not clear what the result would have been if South African bilateral trade with African partners had been taken into account. Third, the authors did not control for the effect of infrastructure, a factor which proved to be crucial in later studies (Limao and Venables, 2001). Fourth, the question addressed by Foroutan and Pritchett is not exactly the same question this chapter is interested in. Foroutan and Pritchett determine whether actual trade is too little given expectations and based on some trade determinants, excluding infrastructure. This chapter is more interested in the future of intra-African trade and considers how better infrastructure would help to increase trade flows among African countries.

The question of interest is the extent to which intra-African trade can be increased if the factors constraining it could be improved. In other words, what is the potential for increasing intra-African trade in a way that fosters economic growth and development of African countries? Many studies based on the gravity model suggest that intra-African trade could be substantially increased if the obstacles that are currently impeding it could be removed. According to the analogy of the gravity model discussed earlier, these obstacles may be discussed under the headings weak "attraction forces" and strong "opposing forces".

1. Weak "attraction forces"

The forces that attract trade include factors which are fixed and not amenable to policy. The main ones usually considered are a country's physical size measured in square kilometres, common language and common history of the countries in the trading bloc. Their specific individual effect on regional trade is difficult to assess, given that they do not seem to have the same effect on trade across regions. For example, evidence based on data covering the period 1996–1998 shows that being a French speaker induces three times more import demand from the West African Economic and Monetary Union (WAEMU), which is a group of countries sharing the same language, French, and the same colonial history (Coulibaly and Fontagné, 2005). In contrast, trade within the Arab Maghreb Union is close to insignificant, despite the relative homogeneity of this group in which all the countries speak Arabic and share Arabic cultural heritage.

The second group of determinants comprises factors that are dynamic. The main ones are economic size measured as a country's gross domestic product (GDP) or population size, and income per capita to proxy for the level of demand.[14] Most empirical studies of international trade find that the size and income per capita variables are positively related to the level of trade. Considering the low level of income in Africa, both aggregate and per capita, it is logical that these variables constrain intra-African trade. While it is clear that increasing incomes in Africa will more likely have a positive effect on trade flows, how to achieve this objective is a much wider question beyond the scope of this report. Therefore, most of the discussion of intra-African trade flows focuses on trade-specific factors, particularly the issue of high trade costs.

There is an argument that African countries trade less because they have similar production structures (Yeats, 1998; Dinka and Kennes, 2007). While this is a valid argument, it should not overshadow other important constraints to intra-African trade. Indeed, even if countries produce the same goods, their production costs are often different. Hence, consumers may have good reasons for buying imported goods relative to similar domestic products. China, for example, has dramatically increased its exports to developed economies, not because it produces goods that are not produced in these countries, but because China produces similar goods at lower cost. Regional trade among African countries producing similar goods can be driven by the same dynamic.

A case in point is trade in agricultural products, particularly food. Although it is poorly recorded in national statistics, cross-border trade in agricultural products has been taking place across Africa over the years despite the fact that many African economies produce agricultural products (Little, 2007). The problem has been that the bulky nature of agricultural trade limits trading over long distances in view of the poor infrastructure and high trading costs, which discourages production and hence intra-African trade in such commodities. This effect has been well documented at the national level and a similar effect obtains at the regional level.[15] Addressing the domestic and regional infrastructure challenges, in addition to lowering trade costs, could pave the way for higher intra-African trade, including trade in agricultural commodities.

2. Strong "opposing forces"

Forces opposed to the expansion of intra-African trade result in high trade costs, which are defined as all costs involved in getting a final good to a final user. High trade costs are mainly due to poor hard and soft infrastructure.

(a) High trade costs: transport, border and behind-border costs

In general, high tariff barriers and other trade costs are the main forces opposed to the expansion of trade. However, with the generalized reduction in trade tariffs over the past years (UNCTAD, 2008a), trade among African countries is to a large extent hampered by trade costs other than tariffs (Njinkeu et al., 2008).[16] Therefore, the discussion below focuses on high trade costs as being the most important factor constraining intra-African trade, as they are higher in Africa than anywhere else. Table 8 illustrates that trading across borders is more cumbersome, slower, and costlier than in most other regions. While not specific to intraregional trade, these figures highlight the multiple obstacles to trade that endure on the continent, despite the fact that Africa is the region that is reforming its trade procedures most rapidly (World Bank, 2009).

Non-tariff trade costs are disaggregated into three main components: transport costs, administrative procedures causing inefficiencies inherent in crossing borders, and other costs incurred beyond the national border.

Transport costs

Transport costs are arguably the most important impediment to intra-African trade. Unfortunately, there are no good measures of transport costs, so many early studies using the gravity model relied on the distance between partner countries to proxy for transport costs, despite the problems associated with the use of such a measure.[17] Recent studies using better measures of transport costs show that they are indeed central to explaining the low level of intra-African trade.

Table 8
Export and import procedures, time and cost for selected regions, 2009

	Number of documents needed for export	Time for export (days)	Cost to export ($ per container)	Documents for import (number)	Time for import (days)	Cost to import ($ per container)
Organization for Economic Cooperation and Development	4.5	10.7	1 069.1	5.1	11.4	1 132.7
East Asia and Pacific	6.7	23.3	902.3	7.1	24.5	948.5
Latin America and Caribbean	6.9	19.7	1 229.8	7.4	22.3	1 384.3
Eastern Europe and Central Asia	7.1	29.7	1 649.1	8.3	31.7	1 822.2
Middle East and North Africa	6.5	23.3	1 024.4	7.6	26.7	1 204.8
Sub-Saharan Africa	7.8	34.7	1 878.8	8.8	41.1	2 278.7

Source: World Bank, 2009.

Note: This information measures procedural requirements for exporting and importing standardized cargo of goods by ocean transport, from the contractual agreement between the two parties to the delivery of goods, along with the time and cost necessary for completion. All documents required for clearance of the goods across the border are also recorded. For exporting goods, procedures range from packing the goods at the factory to their departure from the port of exit. For importing goods, procedures range from the vessel's arrival at the port of entry to the cargo's delivery at the factory warehouse. For more details, consult: http://www.doingbusiness.org/MethodologySurveys/TradingAcrossBorders.aspx.

Econometric estimates find that transport costs in Africa are 136 per cent higher than in other regions and that poor infrastructure only accounts for half of these costs (Limao and Venables, 2001). However, costs vary considerably between countries and products (Amjadi and Yeats, 1995). Not surprisingly, therefore, sub-Saharan Africa is the region with the largest proportion of firms identifying transportation as a major constraint to doing business (World Bank, 2009). In the United Republic of Tanzania and Uganda in the early 2000s, the rate of effective taxation of exports due to transport costs was 40 per cent. This is much higher than the average of 15 per cent for ACP countries.

Using a global sample comprising African and non-African countries, a quantitative analysis of the association between transport costs and trade shows some interesting facts (Limao and Venables, 2001). First, a doubling of the median value of transport costs reduces trade volumes by 45 per cent, illustrating the strong correlation between transport costs and trade volumes. Second, the adverse effects of transport costs are especially acute for landlocked countries where these costs are 50 per cent higher and trade volumes 60 per cent lower than in coastal economies. This is particularly relevant for Africa, which hosts the highest number of landlocked countries. Landlocked countries in Africa were recently found to have freight costs equivalent to between 10 and 25 per cent of the total value of their imports while the global average is of 5.4 per cent (UNCTAD, 2007a). In fact, as tariffs are being lowered around the world, transport costs impose a higher level of effective protection than tariffs do particularly in landlocked countries (Amjadi and Yeats, 1995). Additionally, high transport-related trade costs act as a severe disincentive not only to increased trade but also to FDI flows to landlocked countries (UNCTAD, 2008b).

Inefficiency of border procedures

This is due to breakdowns of the electronic system for document lodging, poor coordination in the inspection of goods between different actors, overly zealous inspection of goods, insufficient opening times at the point of entry, and delays in duty refunds, among others. These procedures impose a heavy cost on intra-African trade mostly through the delays they cause (Gad, 2009). This is particularly so for landlocked countries whose goods must necessarily cross the borders of their neighbouring countries. It is estimated that crossing a transit territory implies an additional 4 per cent increase in trade costs irrespective of the distance covered (Coulibaly and Fontagné, 2005). This is why the efficiency of the customs environment has a significant impact on trade (Njinkeu et al., 2008).

These findings are confirmed by a recent survey of the private sector in eight African countries. More than 85 per cent of the firms in the sample reported that they experienced increased costs due to border controls. Also, more than half of the firms reported lost business due to these controls, and nearly 25 per cent reported lost or damaged cargo (Gad, 2009).

Other costs

Exporters and importers face several additional constraints related to the business environment in their own countries, and these constraints have been found to have a negative impact on the level of trade. Corruption and the lack of transparency and predictability of trade-related operations, for example, increase both the cost and uncertainty of trading (Portugal-Perez and Wilson, 2008). This illustrates the importance for trade of a coherent and predictable economic policy environment.

Political tensions also have a significant negative effect on regional trade (Longo and Sekkat, 2004). This includes harming both the production and transport of goods across borders. When political tensions have a regional character, trade between the conflicting countries is among the key sectors that suffer. A good illustration is the collapse of the East African Community in 1977 (since restored) following political differences between the leaders of the three countries forming the community. As noted in chapter 1, this had a strong negative effect on investment and trade within the region. Following de-integration in East Africa, many firms established there, particularly in Kenya, to produce and sell to the large regional market experienced difficulties. Some closed down while others were forced to curtail their activities. For example, a survey of manufacturing firms carried out in Kenya in the 1990s showed that a number of firms had to operate below half of their capacity as a result of the collapse of the East African community (Himbara, 1994; Mwega and Ndung'u, 2008). In the same connection, political differences could also explain the relatively low level of trade between neighbouring countries in North Africa.

(b) Explaining high trade costs: hard and soft infrastructure

The high trade costs faced by African countries effectively act as a barrier to intra-African trade. While these costs affect Africa's trade in general, their effects are considerably more pronounced on intra-Africa trade than they are on Africa's trade with the rest of the world (Longo and Sekkat, 2004; Njinkeu et al., 2008). At the root of these costs are deficiencies in two principal areas: "hard" and "soft" infrastructure.

Hard infrastructure

The term refers to the physical infrastructure that is often missing or is of poor quality in many African countries. Within this category, poor transport infrastructure is the key constraint to intra-African trade and it is especially detrimental to long-distance trading (Limao and Venables, 2001; Ndulu, 2006). Improving physical infrastructure can therefore have an important effect on raising the levels of intra-African trade. Halving transport costs in a typical landlocked country, for example, can increase the country's trade fivefold (Limao and Venables, 2001).

Among all transport modes, road transport is the most important means of trade between African countries. In a recent survey of businesses in eight African countries, it was found that a large majority of businesses use road transport as their preferred means of transportation, due mainly to the lack of alternatives, notably the inefficiency of existing rail services and the high cost of air transport (Gad, 2009).[18] However, the quality of the road network on the continent is so poor that many countries even within the same RTA remain effectively isolated from each other, let alone between different parts of Africa. Central Africa is a good illustration.

Recent estimates shed new light on how important the effects of road quality on African trade are. Improving the main intra-African road network could generate trade expansion of around $250 billion over a period of 15 years for an investment of $32 billion, including maintenance (Buys et al., 2006). The most important gains from an improvement in road quality can be made by the more isolated countries. It is estimated that from the investment mentioned above, Chad would see a trade increase of 507 per cent; Uganda would see an increase of 741 per cent while Sudan could see an increase of 1027 per cent (Buys et al., 2006). According to a similar study covering WAEMU, paving the road linking Mali to Senegal would increase bilateral trade flows fourfold. Paving the road linking Senegal and Côte d'Ivoire would double bilateral trade flows between these two countries.[19] Overall, regional trade within WAEMU would increase threefold if all intrastate roads linking WAEMU countries were paved (Coulibaly and Fontagné, 2005).

Regional transport infrastructure and the adoption of the policies accompanying it can also help to alleviate the relative isolation of landlocked countries. In Uganda, for example, until the dismantling of the East African Railways, the fact that the country is landlocked had a marginal impact on Uganda's trade. The railway was a regionally managed and relatively cheap mode of transport linking Uganda to the ocean via Kenya. This changed in 1977 when East African Railways was split into national segments managed at the national level. The split reduced the efficiency of the railway as it introduced additional costs pertaining to management, maintenance, border controls and other coordination costs (Atingi-Ego and Kasekende, 2008). As a result, transport costs increased dramatically, reducing Uganda's export competitiveness.

Reliable and effective physical infrastructure does not matter only for transport costs however. Indeed, other forms of efficient and reliable domestic services infrastructure – including telecommunications, financial intermediation and logistics – have also been found to be positively correlated with intraregional trade (Njinkeu et al., 2008). Overall, infrastructure deficits in Africa have been estimated to lower firm productivity by around 40 per cent (Foster, 2008).

Soft infrastructure

Important as improvements in hard infrastructures are, they represent only a part of the solution to the constraints limiting intra-African trade. Many other issues, which together can be termed "soft" infrastructure, impact on trade costs. These include the policy and regulatory environment, the transparency and predictability of trade and business administration, and the quality of the business environment more generally. Improvements in soft infrastructure are necessary in order to reap the full rewards of better hard infrastructure (Portugal-Perez and Wilson, 2008). According to some analysts, soft infrastructure issues such as customs procedures and regulatory environment have been identified as the main obstacles to intra-African trade (Njinkeu et al., 2008). In Angola, modernization of customs has cut processing time and customs revenue has increased by 150 per cent. In Ghana, customs clearing time at the airport has been reduced from three days to four hours on average as a result of the adoption of a more efficient technology and simplification of procedures. Revenue from airport traffic has increased by 30 per cent. Similar reforms in Mozambique resulted in 58 per cent increase in customs revenue. Through its Automated System for Customs Data (ASYCUDA) programme, UNCTAD has been at the forefront of the effort to help Africa modernize its customs administration (see box 2).

Transport policy provides one example of the way "soft" infrastructural issues affect transport costs. In addition to the effect of the poor quality of physical infrastructure, high transport costs in Africa are also due to poorly designed national regulations that stifle competition between transport service providers (Amjadi and Yeats, 1995). As a result, the strong informal and formal protection from competition enjoyed by transporters in many African countries allows them to continue charging very high prices despite the fairly low costs they face. In sub-Saharan Africa, road freight tariffs are in the range of $0.04–0.14 per ton and per kilometre compared to $0.01–0.04 per ton and per kilometre in other developing regions (Foster, 2008). This problem has been found to be especially acute in landlocked countries (Portugal-Perez and Wilson, 2008).

Similarly, the costs incurred at borders and ports are not only a function of the quality of physical infrastructure found there. In fact, border costs are often related to weak institutions which create costs through irregular payments

---

Box 2. ASYCUDA in Africa

ASYCUDA was first implemented in Mali and Mauritania in the early 1980s. Over the past 25 years, it has been subsequently installed in 38 African countries and implementation is expected to reach 40 countries in 2009. The system is currently used in more than 300 customs offices across the continent, where it processes more than 6 million customs declarations per year. The installation of ASYCUDA is performed together with the establishment of trade facilitation and regional harmonization measures. A direct consequence of customs modernization is an accrued transparency of the overall customs operations which leads to an increase in customs revenue.

The recent introduction in the system of modern customs techniques such as Direct Trader Input and Risk Management has given a boost to trade, especially in the COMESA region. Transit issues are crucial for the development of landlocked developing countries (LLDCs). Thus, through ASYCUDA, the computerization of all transit operations in countries such as Botswana, Zambia and Zimbabwe has significantly contributed to a more effective control of cargo movement in the southern corridors.

Recently, in addition to the existing three regional support centers for COMESA (Lusaka), ECOWAS (Lomé) and the Southern and Eastern African Technical ASYCUDA (SEATAC, Dar es Salaam), a fourth regional center for CEMAC countries has been funded by the EU and will be located in Bangui (Central African Republic). It will focus on the development of a regional transit management system using ASYCUDAWorld and its implementation on two transit corridors: Douala (Cameroon)–Bangui (Central African Republic); and Douala–N'djamena (Chad). In addition, a homogenization of national systems to the same ASYCUDA release will be performed.

Source: UNCTAD secretariat.

(corruption). The lack of transparency in border procedures and customs administration increases uncertainty and discourages trade (Njinkeu et al, 2008). Table 8 shows that importing and exporting goods still require more time and a greater number of procedures in Africa than in other regions. Remedying this will require not only greater resources to improve border efficiency but also a simplification of trade procedures and strong political will to curb corruption and hassling at border posts and roadblocks.

Having in place the right policies and regulations also matters behind borders and has an impact on intra-African trade. Most generally, the quality of the business environment and economic policy in general are important determinants of whether or not trading opportunities will be seized by economic agents. The dramatic growth of exports from Mauritius from $89 million in 1970 to $2.8 billion in 2000 is partly attributed to trade facilitation measures, which reduced the cost and risk of exporting (Milner et al., 2008). Accordingly, some estimates suggest that an increase of 1 per cent in the quality of economic policy yields 0.6 to 1 per cent increase in intra-African trade (Longo and Sekkat, 2004).[20]

The implementation of many of these measures requires coordination at the regional level. For example, the dependence of landlocked countries on their neighbours' trade infrastructure implies that they should cooperate to build and maintain it. Besides, financing regional infrastructure is expensive, so it would make economic sense to share the cost of financing regional infrastructure among the countries concerned.[21] For example, Burundi, Rwanda and the United Republic of Tanzania have agreed to pool their resources in order to finance the construction of a regional railway network crossing all three countries. The new network, the first railway to operate in Burundi and Rwanda, will be linked to East Africa's Central Corridor railway going all the way to the Indian Ocean port of Dar-es-Salaam (Muwanga, 2009). This railway network is expected to substantially reduce trade costs in East Africa once completed.

3. The particular challenge of landlocked countries

Resource-scarce landlocked countries host 35 per cent of Africa's population. This is a very high concentration considering that the proportion outside Africa is only 1 per cent of the population (Collier and O'Connell, 2008). The presence of so many poor landlocked countries in Africa could have an overall negative effect on trade because these countries are confronted with particular challenges that coastal countries do not have. But why is being landlocked such an important constraint to trade in Africa when it is not in Europe, for example? Why is trade with Burundi, a small African landlocked country, suffering from the country's geographical position when trade with Switzerland, a small European landlocked country, is not?

The problem with landlocked countries is not necessarily related to their geographical position. Switzerland does not necessarily need to cross its coastal neighbours (France, Germany and Italy) to trade because these countries constitute a large part of its market. In contrast, Burundi relies on the poor roads, railways and ports of the United Republic of Tanzania, Rwanda, Uganda and Kenya to reach the coast because Burundi's main import and export markets are outside Africa.[22] Landlocked countries' trading costs are particularly high because these countries' trade is conditioned on crossing borders and paying the price of their neighbours' poor soft and hard infrastructure, in addition to their own.

In addition to raising trading costs, being landlocked increases uncertainty, which imposes an additional cost. As the time to markets increases, importers and exporters have a weak control over market parameters, including movements in prices and exchange rates. Hence, importers and exporters in landlocked countries cannot predict with some reasonable degree of certainty their trade costs and hence the profitability of their activities. This has a negative effect on economic activity. Moreover, the fear of supply interruptions due to market and transport uncertainty forces producers in landlocked countries to invest in large stocks of inputs, which increases the cost of production and reduces competitiveness (Fafchamps et al, 2000). A firm survey in Burundi, for example, showed that firms using imported raw materials keep very large stocks of imported inputs. At any time, this stock represents, on average, 87 per cent of total raw material needs for a year (Nkurunziza and Ngaruko, 2008).

In Malawi, another African landlocked country, the share of inventory investment in total investment in the manufacturing sector was 35.44 per cent during the period 1985–1989 and it has remained high. The main reasons were foreign exchange constraints and high transport costs. The average transport cost, including insurance, represents 47 per cent of the total import cost. Due to poor domestic infrastructure, trucking cartels, high taxation on the transport sector and limitations on the operations of foreign vehicles, internal transport costs in Malawi are in the range of $0.065–$ 0.075 per kilometre. These are about two to three times the costs in South Africa, a country with good quality roads and competitive transport sector (Chipeta and Mkandawire, 2008).

Being landlocked does not necessarily imply poor economic performance, even in Africa, because policy choices can alleviate the effects of this natural constraint. Over the period 1960–2000, Malawi recorded a level of growth in real GDP per worker of 1.67 per cent per year, which was far higher than the average for both sub-Saharan Africa and Latin America and the Caribbean. Most particularly, between 1960 and 1979, Malawi saw the most sustained growth rate in real per worker GDP, averaging 3 per cent per year. This was a period of large-scale state investments such as infrastructure building and rural development. During this period, economic controls were mild and they did not hurt the stability of the macroeconomic environment. This in turn encouraged private and public savings as well as physical capital accumulation. Indeed, physical capital per worker grew at a rate of 3.12 per cent per year during this period.

However, these trends could not be sustained as they were reversed in the ensuing period (1980–2000) following a series of largely external shocks that hit the economy in the late 1970s.[23] The adoption of a structural adjustment programme and its bias against the state changed the policies that had successfully produced these high rates of growth. The response was a collapse in investment and increased macroeconomic instability. Real growth in GDP per worker dropped to a mere 0.16 per cent during the period (Chipeta and Mkandawire, 2008).

Overdependence of African landlocked economies on their neighbours suggests two possible policy options, particularly in the area of trade. First, landlocked countries should be the champions of the regional integration movement in order to benefit from the structures established for regional negotiations within which they could influence their neighbours' policies towards these countries. Second, landlocked countries should consider developing knowledge economies, which are less dependent on neighbouring coastal economies. In contrast to goods-based trade, which is bulky and too dependent on land transport infrastructure, trade in specific services could help to circumvent the current physical infrastructure constraint facing landlocked economies. Such services could include document translation, electronic document processing, accounting, telephone-based customer service, etc.[24] However, for landlocked countries to reap the opportunities offered by this growing trade, they will need to modernize their education sector, build reliable telecommunication infrastructure and stabilize their macroeconomic environment, among others.

D. Future of intra-African trade

The evolution of intra-African trade in the foreseeable future will depend on a number of processes taking place both within and outside Africa. Generally, African economies are being affected by the same factors affecting the world economy, the most prominent currently being the global economic crisis. As Africa's global export markets shrink, the continent's export revenue will drop. Therefore, it is even more urgent for African countries to take steps to develop their intraregional trade in order to offset losses from their traditional export markets.

1. Deepening regional integration

RTAs have been a feature of Africa ever since the world's first RTA was created in Southern Africa in 1910. There are now too many regional economic integration units and their pace and breadth in terms of developing intra-African trade is variable and will no doubt continue to be so. The political commitment to the establishment of an African Common Market by 2023 is still on the table but achieving this objective will most probably require prior rationalization of the existing schemes (ECA, 2006a).

There are a number of encouraging signs suggesting that the political commitment to greater integration is currently strong. In East Africa, for example, the East African Community has recently expanded with the inclusion of Burundi and Rwanda. The benefits from joining for the two landlocked countries whose economies are highly dependent on EAC's coastal countries (Kenya and the United Republic of Tanzania) are obvious. These two countries stand to benefit if liberalization within the community is not frustrated by political considerations, as has happened before.

More importantly, if the current initiative to merge some of the continent's largest RTAs becomes reality, it certainly will accelerate intra-African trade. Indeed, it was announced in late 2008 that COMESA, EAC, and SADC planned to merge to form a free trade area. The resulting trade bloc would create a free trade area covering 527 million people with a combined GDP of $624 billion (International Centre for Trade and Sustainable Development (ICTSD), 2008). This would be an important stepping stone towards the formation of an African Common Market.

2. Processes shaping Africa's integration into the global trading system

At the international stage, there are several ongoing developments which will certainly play an important role in determining the future of intra-African trade and the continent's integration into the world trading system. The most prominent now are the negotiations for EPAs between Africa and the EU. Other important developments are the WTO Doha Round of negotiations, AGOA, TIFA and the recent rise of China as a major player in world trade. Each of these is briefly discussed below.

(a) Negotiations under the EPAs

Sub-Saharan African countries tend to export heavily to Europe (see table 4). Until 2000, this trade had been regulated by the Yaoundé and then Lomé conventions, which granted products ACP countries preferential access, on a non-reciprocal basis, to EU markets. This arrangement, however, was not WTO-compatible and was seen as having achieved limited success in terms of promoting accelerated development in ACP countries. Following the Cotonou Agreement of 2000, steps have been taken to redefine the trade relations between ACP countries and the EU in a way that would be both WTO-compatible and more conducive to economic development. Accordingly, the EU is negotiating EPAs with ACP regions.

EPAs are essentially RTAs between the EU and regional groupings of ACP countries. At present, none of the four African groupings has completed negotiations to establish an EPA with the EU. Instead, several countries — such as Côte d'Ivoire, Ghana and Cameroon — have established interim EPAs with the EU pending the establishment of the regional EPAs. These negotiations are of crucial importance to African trade. They concern not only market access to Africa's largest export market, but also have wider implications for Africa's economic future.

Information in draft EPAs under negotiation shows that they cover a wide array of topics, including some that developing countries have resisted discussing in WTO, such as investment, competition policy and government procurement. Moreover, unlike the previous agreements, EPAs require African countries to offer reciprocal market access to EU products, after a transitional period that varies between EPAs.[25] Accordingly, fears have been expressed that EPAs could force African markets to liberalize faster and in more areas than would be good for them. This fear is not helped by the perception that the EU negotiates from a position of strength, being not only an important export market but also a major source of aid to African countries.

Given that strengthening regional integration is one of the main mandates of the EPAs, African countries should take full advantage of this. EPAs could influence African regional trade through their development component. It specifies the main areas of focus of the parties to the agreement in order to meet developmental and regional integration objectives. The development cooperation component is designed to help countries alleviate the costs inherent in entering into EPAs. EPAs should also help African economies to acquire the capabilities required to reap the full benefits of the new opportunities that are expected to result from improvements in trade.

The discussion in this chapter has shown that intra-African trade is considerably limited by poor or lacking infrastructure, soft and hard, and the high trade costs that this creates. Therefore, infrastructure improvement should be among the key priorities of these EPAs. Helping Africa to put in place the hard and soft infrastructure needed to strengthen the economic integration among African countries could pave the way for higher FDI flows and more intra-African trade, resulting in higher rates of economic growth.

African countries should take a proactive stance by analyzing and identifying their needs in terms of both hard and soft infrastructure support. This analysis should serve as a basis for cooperation with other parties to the EPA on the allocation of resources at both the national and regional levels. These resources should help to foster a type of integration that helps to ease trade and investment constraints within Africa, rather than focusing solely on Africa's integration with the EU (Dinka and Kennes, 2007). The regional dimension of this assistance is of particular importance for Africa's many landlocked countries whose access to markets depends, to a large extent, on their neighbouring countries. At the regional level, EPA interventions should be integrated within NEPAD's spatial development programme.

Clearer and more binding commitments within existing interim EPAs would reduce uncertainty about the type and levels of future assistance. This in turn would help determine the extent to which African countries or regions can be expected to undertake the type of large investments required to develop their infrastructure. This has led African ministers of trade and finance to urge the EU to provide adequate and predictable resources, notably for the development of physical infrastructure, regulatory capacity, and national and regional interconnectivity (AU, 2008).

A related issue is the EU's commitment under the Aid for Trade initiative. The EU has been a big contributor and its trade-specific commitments have focused on assistance in the area of negotiation and implementation of trade rules. Other Aid for Trade areas, including trade-related infrastructure development, also currently benefit from important amounts of assistance from EU countries. Continuing this trend in the future will be essential for Africa to meet its large and long-term investments needs for infrastructure development (South Centre, 2008). The expected effect of EPAs on Africa's trade would be better understood if the commitments made under the various categories of development cooperation could be specified.

(b) Other processes with a potentially strong effect on intra-African trade

Other processes that will more likely shape the future of Africa's trade are briefly discussed below.

Doha Round of negotiations

Although the WTO negotiations are all but stalled at the moment, future developments there will likely continue to shape Africa's integration into the world economy. Notably, whether or not the Doha Round yields a favourable agreement regarding market access for agricultural commodities could have a sizeable influence on African trade. In the absence of such a deal, and if obstacles to intra-African trade are further reduced, an increasingly important proportion of primary product exports could be directed at intra-African trade. Higher investment in agriculture and agro industries would be required if Africa is to derive maximum benefit from increased intra-African trade in primary products.

The African Growth and Opportunity Act

AGOA is another agreement that could have an important effect on Africa's regional trade. By 2008, 40 African countries were eligible to benefit from the AGOA agreement, which offers preferential market access to the United States market for certain products; e.g. 27 countries were eligible to receive apparel benefits. From AGOA's inception in 2000 until 2007, Africa's exports to the United States tripled to $67.4 billion, and over 98 per cent of these exports entered duty free (Office of the United States Trade Representative, 2008).[26] African apparel exporters to the United States were given a new boost when the United States Congress repealed AGOA's "abundant supply" provision in October 2008 (Whitaker Group, 2008). This measure and further relaxation of AGOA's rules of origin could help increase intra-African trade if manufacturers are allowed to source their inputs from anywhere in Africa.[27]

Trade and Investment Framework Agreements with the United States

In addition to multilateral agreements, a number of African countries and regional integration groupings have negotiated or are negotiating bilateral trade and investment framework agreements with the United States. By the end of 2008, there were TIFAs with COMESA, WAEMU, EAC, Algeria, Ghana, Liberia,

Mauritius, Mozambique, Nigeria, Rwanda and Tunisia.[28] As in the case of AGOA, these agreements could impact intra-African trade if they allow their signatories to source inputs from other African countries, including non-signatory countries. Given that they have an investment component, the agreements could also attract more FDI to Africa, which could eventually increase production and intra-African trade.

The emergence of China as a world economic power

China is affecting the world economy in an unprecedented way. The deepening of China's economic relations with Africa could have a positive long-lasting impact on Africa's trade, including intra-African trade. China's involvement in infrastructure development, for example, is filling a gap that will most likely increase domestic and regional market integration in Africa. As the discussions in this chapter have shown, this is badly needed if Africa is to integrate its economies and substantially increase its intra-African trade. Moreover, the importance of Chinese FDI, particularly in non-traditional areas such as agriculture, could have a notable impact on African economies and their intraregional trade flows if agricultural commodities are produced cheaply and at a large scale. China has recently invested in the production of food crops in Kenya, Zambia and Zimbabwe, for example (Sheridan, 2007). This has boosted local production and trade, contributing to improvements in food security in Africa. Ultimately, Chinese current involvement in Africa has diversified Africa's economic options, a positive development for the continent. It is up to African countries to wisely use this opportunity to advance their development agenda. Most particularly, considering China's experience with rapid industrial development, African countries should take advantage of the Chinese presence to alleviate their commodity dependence by rebuilding Africa's shattered industrial sector through higher local processing and other forms of value addition.

E. Conclusion

Analysis of the trends and patterns of intra-African trade and a review of empirical studies explaining its level and potential reveal a number of stylized facts. First, although the aggregate level of intra-African trade is low in comparison with other regions, intra-African trade is important for many African countries taken individually. Second, over three quarters of intra-African trade takes place within regional trading blocs, highlighting their importance. Third, in every region, trade takes place around a few influential countries. This suggests the existence of "trade poles" that could become development poles. Fourth, the pattern of trade within Africa and between Africa and the rest of the world is different. While manufactured products dominate intra-African exports, exports to the rest of the world are mainly primary commodities. Also, whereas Africa's exports to the rest of the world are highly concentrated around a few products, intra-African trade is much more diversified. Fifth, the difficulties facing landlocked African economies are particularly severe, given that, in most cases, these countries' trade is overly dependent on relatively poor neighbours. Hence, landlocked countries in Africa cannot benefit from positive neighbourhood effects, as observed elsewhere.

The analysis of the reason why intra-African trade is so low relative to potential reveals the importance of excessively high transport costs due to poor hard and soft infrastructure. This is particularly the case for landlocked countries, which are constrained by their own poor infrastructure as well as their neighbours'. Inefficient and multiple border procedures, political instability and unpredictability, as well as uncertainty, of trade policies also hamper intra-African trade by raising trade costs, despite remarkable progress achieved in these areas over the recent past. Moreover, processes such as the EPA negotiations, the WTO Doha Round of multilateral trade negotiations, AGOA — as well as recent bilateral and multilateral agreements between Africa and economic powerhouses such as the United States and China — are expected to have a notable effect on the future of intra-African trade.

Chapter 3

Intra-African investment

Trade and investment are two sides of the same coin. As discussed in chapter 1, beside the allocation effect of regional integration, increasing investment and trade is the main reason countries decide to form regional economic blocs. Indeed, the expansion of markets following the formation of economic blocs invites more trade, which in turn requires more investment. Moreover, much of current production, trade and international financial flows are shaped by transnational corporations (TNCs). They integrate goods and services, and factor markets across national boundaries, illustrating the close link between investment and trade. Integration in the corporate sector by TNC initiatives on the one hand and government efforts at regional and subregional economic and financial integration on the other reinforce each other.

Despite this link between trade and investment, very little has been written on intra-African investment. This could be due to the fact that, until very recently, the flows of intra-African investment had been negligible. As later discussions will show, the situation is changing now. A few African countries are becoming major investors in other African countries.

There is a severe data limitation that does not allow the analysis of intra-African investment similar to the format of chapter 2 on intra-African trade. In fact, it is almost impossible to assess the level, scope, significance and direction of foreign investment from Africa, because no African country other than South Africa keeps data on outward FDI stock and flows that can be meaningfully aggregated and compared. Furthermore, it is difficult to determine the extent to which the investments are genuinely from domestic corporations in the countries concerned, as opposed to local affiliates of developed country TNCs.

Given the data constraint, this chapter has a very limited scope. Its main objective is to start a debate on intra-African investment, as the issue is gaining prominence. The chapter has two parts. The first highlights some stylized facts about intra-African investment. These include the level and relative importance of intra-African investment, its geographical distribution in terms of origin and destination, and its sectoral composition. The second part presents the illustrative cases of West African and Southern African intra-African investments. These are the most important foreign investment actors within the continent.

A. Some stylized facts on intra-African investment

1. Intra-African investment flows are low but increasing

Africa has traditionally relied on foreign investments from outside the continent. As a result, it has entered or is in the process of entering into investment agreements with countries and regions mostly outside of Africa. For example, negotiations for investment agreements between Africa's RTAs and the EU have been proposed in the context of EPAs. On 16 July 2008, SACU signed a TIDCA with the United States. The United States has also entered into TIFAs with several RTAs and African countries. By the end of 2008, the United States had signed TIFAs with COMESA, WAEMU, EAC, and eight African countries (see chapter 2).

Over-reliance on external investment is the result of African countries' inability to mobilize sizable financial resources to invest in other African countries until very recently. In the period 2002–2004, intra-African FDI was estimated at only $2 billion annually on average, which represented about 13 per cent of total inward FDI (UNCTAD, 2006b).[29] In comparison, intraregional FDI in countries from the Association of South-east Asian Nations (ASEAN) is estimated at 30 per cent of total FDI. In 2007 in Africa, the flow of intra-African investment amounted to $6 billion, raising the accumulated stock to $73 billion (UNCTAD, 2008g).

The low level of intraregional FDI in Africa can be attributed to several factors. Key among these is the lack of adequate transport and communication infrastructure, skilled labour, and weak economic links and contacts among investors within the region. Moreover, there is a strong correlation between foreign and domestic investment because foreign investors view the behaviour of the local investors as important information signals. The low level of domestic investment in Africa is therefore partly responsible for the limited intraregional investment. Indeed, it has been found that private domestic investment drives foreign investment (Ndikumana and Verick, 2008).

Intraregional FDI is geographically concentrated among the more developed African countries, mainly in Southern Africa and North Africa. Poor quality and performance of production and human capital — including lack of technology know-how or information originating from the region — lead other African country firms to seek FDI abroad, traditionally in developed countries (Europe and the United States). However, this is changing relatively fast.

The phenomenal growth of economies in different parts of the developing world, coupled with the recent boom in commodities, has created new and powerful financial actors from Asia, Latin America and the Middle East. These actors have accumulated the necessary financial and technological capabilities to invest abroad, so they are looking for new investment opportunities. In absolute terms, outward FDI flows from developing countries increased from an annual average of $65 billion in the 1990s to over $250 billion in 2007. Their outward FDI stock level in 2007 was over $4 trillion. In addition to FDI flows and stocks, data on cross-border mergers and acquisitions (M&As), greenfield investment expansion projects also confirm the growing significance of TNCs from developing countries (UNCTAD, 2008g).

Intense competition for investment opportunities and a more positive attitude towards FDI from developing countries are changing the traditional international investment landscape.[30] Africa is embracing these emerging foreign investors and the continent is looking more and more to non-traditional sources of foreign investment to raise funds. Countries such as China, India, Malaysia and Singapore are now among the top 20 investors in Africa as reflected in the distribution of the stock of FDI per country of origin covering the period 2003–2007 (see table 9).

The positive attitude towards investment from other developing countries is producing important results with respect to intra-African investment. A number of African TNCs are quickly spreading throughout the continent and they are often displacing more traditional sources of FDI. For example, as discussed later in this chapter, West African banks have been aggressively taking over domestic banks in several African countries where Western interests had been controlling the banking sector for a long time. As a result, intra-African investment flows are on the rise. South Africa is the single most important African source of the continent's stock of foreign investment (table 9).[31]

The implications for Africa as host and home to FDI are important in terms of attracting new inflows of FDI into Africa's economies. Moreover, these changes are also important in order to secure the participation of TNCs to add momentum to the regional integration efforts. With the current downturn in the world economy, encouraging intra-African investment could help to counteract the weakening of financial flows to Africa from Europe and the United States. This strategic change will particularly help the small and structurally weak African countries which have been too dependent on flows from developed countries.

Table 9

Percentage shares of the top 20 investors in Africa as reported by investing economies, 2003–2007 averages

Rank	Country of origin	Shares in total inward FDI stock in Africa
	Developed economies	79.6
	Developing economies	20.2
	South-east Europe and Commonwealth of Independent States	0.2
1	United Kingdom	21.2
2	United States	19.4
3	France	15.4
4	South Africa	5.9
5	Germany	4.8
6	Singapore	4.4
7	Switzerland	4.3
8	Norway	3.7
9	India	3.6
10	Canada	2.9
11	Japan	2.7
12	Malaysia	2.6
13	Sweden	2.0
14	China	1.8
15	Portugal	1.2
16	Denmark	0.9
17	Taiwan Province of China	0.8
18	Netherland	0.5
19	Morocco	0.4
20	Republic of Korea	0.4
	Others	1.2

Source: UNCTAD, FDI/TNC database.

2. Geographical distribution of intra-African FDI

Although the growth of aggregate African foreign investment has been less spectacular than the global level, intra-African investment has become a very important source of investment for a few African countries. This is particularly the case in Southern Africa, given the prominence of South Africa as the main source of intra-African foreign investment in Africa. In this light, countries such as Botswana, Madagascar, Malawi and Mozambique benefit from their proximity to South Africa (Odenthal, 2001). As shown in table 10, Uganda also has a significant share of African foreign investment in its total foreign investment.

Table 10
Intraregional FDI in Africa, various years

Country	Period average/ year	Source region ($ million) Africa	World	Share of Africa in World (%)
FDI inflows				
Cape Verde	2004–2006	0.2	84.7	0.2
Egypt	2004–2006	8.4	8 772.2	0.1
Ethiopia	1992–1994	0.1	7.0	1.6
	2002–2004	37.3	421.7	8.8
Madagascar	2005–2007	25.0	459.1	5.5
Mauritius	1994–1996	0.9	25.1	3.8
	2004–2006	3.8	129.4	2.9
Morocco	1996–1998	20.3	664.7	3.1
	2004–2006	9.9	2 348.8	0.4
Mozambique	2004–2006	86.1	168.8	51.0
Tunisia	1998–2000	8.5	605.3	1.4
	2005–2007	47.3	1 902.3	2.5
Inward FDI stock				
Botswana	1997	769.7	1 280.2	60.1
	2005	183.8	806.3	22.8
Madagascar	2002	43.0	165.5	26.0
	2006	326.8	932.4	35.0
Malawi	2000	103.6	357.7	29.0
	2004	151.5	562.3	26.9
Morocco	2006	234.7	29 238.7	0.8
South Africa	1990	183.8	9 210.4	2.0
	2000	301.1	43 451.0	0.7
	2006	584.5	87 765.0	0.7
Uganda	2003	249.4	1 358.8	18.4

Source: UNCTAD, FDI/TNC database.

As the case study of South Africa shows in section 3, the country's investments are not limited to Southern Africa, however. The country has invested in every region of the continent and this is not surprising. South Africa is the strongest economy in Africa where it represents almost a quarter of the continent's GDP. Moreover, the sophisticated nature of the South African financial sector has allowed the country to collect financial resources from the rest of the continent in the form of portfolio flows, which South Africa has been sending out in the form of FDI (more details in section 3).

Most recently, Nigeria has also contributed significantly to the growing importance of intra-African investment, particularly portfolio investment. As a result of the consolidation of the banking sector in Nigeria in 2005, the country now has financial institutions that are solid enough to seek opportunities for expansion across Africa and beyond. A few Nigerian banks have opened branches in European and American financial centres in the last three years. However, the most remarkable expansion has occurred in Africa, where Nigerian banks have acquired interests in several countries throughout sub-Saharan Africa, mainly through mergers and acquisitions (see section 3).

The network of intra-African investment is different from the one in ASEAN or Southern Common Market (MERCOSUR) countries in one important way. Unlike these regions, the low level of skills and underdeveloped technological capabilities do not lend themselves to intraregional corporate integration. Only South Africa is in a position to undertake significant financial and technological transfers. Other important African investors include Mauritius, which accounted for 15 per cent of total FDI inflows in Madagascar and 23 per cent in Mozambique during the period 2004–2006).[32] Kenya invested 10 per cent of Uganda's FDI during fiscal years 2000–2002, while Egypt invested 19 per cent of Algeria's inward investment in the period 1999–2001 (UNCTAD, 2008f).

3. Importance of intra-African M&As relative to other forms of investment (FDI and greenfield)

Data on cross-border M&As point to trends similar to FDI, but show a larger share of intraregional investments than in FDI flows or stock. Greenfield investments, which are a typical mode of investment in Africa, are still mainly concluded by non-African countries. According to the number of such deals in Africa, less than a tenth was concluded by African countries during 2003–2007 (table 11).

Table 11

Cross-border M&As in Africa, 1987–2008

Mode of FDI	Period	Acquiring/investing region		Africa's share in world (%)
		World	Africa	
Cross-border M&As *(number of deals)*				
	1987–2008	2 456	773	31
	1987–1994	2 999	118	39
	1995–1999	832	251	30
	2000–2004	617	203	33
	2005–2008	708	201	28
Cross-border M&As *(value in $ millions)*				
	1987–2008	170 155	47 764	28
	1987–1994	5 960	1 832	31
	1995–1999	32 319	19 840	61
	2000–2004	38 964	6 517	17
	2005–2008	92 911	19 575	21
Greenfield investments *(number of deals)*				
	2003–2007	1 939	149	8

Source: UNCTAD, FDI/TNC database.

Depending on sectors, the share of Africa in total cross-border M&A sales in Africa ranges between 17 per cent and 58 per cent. Greenfield investments, in contrast, are rather small. Only the financial sector attracted greenfield investments from Africa representing more than 20 per cent of total greenfield investments in the period 2003–2007 (table 12). This shows the relative importance of M&A vis-à-vis other forms of foreign investment.

4. Sectoral composition of intra-African foreign investments

Information contained in table 12 gives a broad picture of the sectoral composition of intra-African investment relative to foreign investment from outside Africa.

The first message from the table is that intra-African investment favours some sectors. It is highest in the services sector, where it accounts for 36 per cent of deals carried out in Africa, followed by manufacturing (30 per cent) and then the primary sector (26 per cent). The reason may be that intra-African investment favours smaller projects in services and manufacturing, given the relatively small size of investors and recipients. In contrast, investment from outside Africa is highest in the primary sector, where it accounts for 74 per cent of all deals over the period 1987–2008. Investments in this sector are usually large and, in the case of mining, highly capital-intensive, using sophisticated technologies. These

Table 12

Cross-border M&As (1987–2008) and greenfield investment projects (2003–2007) in Africa, by sector/industry of the seller and by investing region
(Number of deals)

Sector/industry of the target country	M&As in Africa by acquiring region, 1987–2008			Greenfield investments in Africa by source region, 2003–2007		
	World	*Africa*	*Africa's share in world (%)*	*World*	*Africa*	*Africa's share in world (%)*
Total	**2 456**	**773**	**31**	**1 939**	**149**	**8**
Primary	*638*	*164*	*26*	*285*	*11*	*4*
Agriculture, hunting, forestry and fishing	32	6	19	..	..	..
Mining, quarrying and petroleum	606	158	26	285	11	4
Manufacturing	*716*	*216*	*30*	*853*	*57*	*7*
Food, beverages and tobacco	159	40	25	110	11	10
Textiles, clothing and leather	37	15	41	61	6	10
Wood and wood products	24	14	58	20	3	15
Chemicals and chemical products	138	42	30	81	2	2
Rubber and plastic products	26	10	38	23	1	4
Non-metallic mineral products	63	16	25	33	6	18
Metals and metal products	62	16	26	207	14	7
Machinery and equipment	45	17	38	46	-	-
Electrical and electronic equipment	52	15	29	88	5	6
Motor vehicles and other transport equipment	46	8	17	141	4	3
Others	64	23	36	43	5	12
Services	*1 102*	*393*	*36*	*801*	*81*	*10*
Hotels and restaurants	53	14	26	105	8	8
Transport, storage and communications	202	68	34	180	11	6
Finance	307	128	42	190	45	24
Business services	249	84	34	304	17	6
Others	291	99	34	22	-	-

Source: UNCTAD, FDI/TNC database.

types of investments are beyond the reach of most African countries. In fact, in the mining sector, which is the largest FDI recipient, intraregional FDI is confined to South African mining TNCs only.

These figures suggest a form of specialization between African and non-African investors. Non-African investors are usually TNCs interested in producing goods in a host country and selling them abroad (non-market-seeking FDI). These TNCs normally invest in big projects, given their financial and technological capabilities. On the other hand, with the exception of large South African firms, African foreign investors target relatively small projects and use relatively accessible technologies. The factors that drive African investors to invest in other African countries include (a) the need to avoid overdependence on the home market; (b) the rising costs of production in the home economy (this is one reason why Mauritius delocalized to Madagascar); (c) pressure from domestic and global competition; and (d) opportunities in host countries, such as privatization of state-owned enterprises. Most of this investment is in consumer products and services (UNCTAD, 2006b). Indeed, table 12 shows that the highest shares of intra-African investment deals are in consumer products sectors, which are less technology-intensive. These are wood and wood products, textiles, clothing and leather. Financial services come second, reflecting recent progress in Africa's financial sector. Geographical proximity and cultural affinity as well as regional integration schemes facilitate investment from within Africa (UNCTAD, 2009). These investors enjoy an information advantage relative to non-African investors, who are constrained by a severe information deficit on Africa (Asiedu, 2002).

The second message relates to the particularly low figure of intra-African investment in agriculture. It is striking that African foreign investors account for only 19 per cent of total investment deals in the agriculture sector, the second-lowest share after "motor vehicles and other transport equipment." The relative abundance of arable land in several African countries combined with predominantly traditional methods of farming in the continent would suggest that the sector should attract more foreign investment from Africa. One possible reason could be the sensitivity surrounding land property rights. Many Africans consider land as a cultural asset, so they may not like to see it in the hands of foreign investors, including those from other African countries. The fear of losing control over land is one of the reasons why many countries are dragging their feet implementing the "right of establishment" clause and its extension to the agriculture sector in integration treaties.[33]

Given the cultural importance of land in African societies, it is not realistic to envisage that private sale of land should be the only option to attract foreign investment in agriculture. Promoting long-term lease arrangements could be another way of encouraging foreign investment in agriculture. Implementing this measure would require setting up the appropriate legal framework governing such contracts.

B. Case studies:
West, North and South African investments in Africa

Intra-African investments come from three main poles. The West African pole, dominated by Nigeria, has developed recently and is very active in mergers and acquisitions in Africa's banking sector. The Northern pole comprises the Libyan Arab Jamahiriya, Egypt and Morocco. Since the end of apartheid, South Africa has been the major player in intra-African trade and investment. However, most recently, banks from West Africa (Nigeria and Togo) have become active investors, particularly in M&As in the banking industry. North African investments across Africa are also gaining importance. This section uses the limited information available to briefly present these trends in intra-African investment.

1. West African investments in Africa's banking sector

In recent years, Nigerian banks have expanded their activities abroad, both inside and outside of Africa. As of September 2008, it was reported that 10 of the 24 licensed commercial banks in Nigeria own at least one fully-fledged licensed bank in a foreign country (Onwuamaeze, 2008). The Nigerian banking sector has become a major player in African finance following a radical consolidation undertaken in 2005. Under the new regulations, banks had to have a minimum capital of 25 billion naira in order not to lose their licenses. As a result, the fragmented banking sector saw its number of banks falling from 89 to 25 institutions. The banks that survived this consolidation drive are now stronger and more viable than before. Coincidentally, consolidation took place at a time of high oil prices and windfalls from Nigerian oil exports, which further boosted the holdings of the country's banks.

As a consequence of the revitalization of the Nigerian banking sector, Nigerian banks now play a central role in Africa's financial system. In the 2008 ranking of Africa's largest banks, 9 of the first 20 banks were Nigerian. Nigeria has become by far the second most important country in African banking following South Africa, which has fewer but larger institutions. In 2008, Nigerian banks accounted for over 25 per cent of African bank capital and seven Nigerian banks are now part of the small number of African banks with capital of over $1 billion (African Business, 2008a).

Banks in Nigeria distinguish themselves not only by their size but also by the quality of their service provision. Nigerian banks were well represented in the recent Africa Banker Awards, winning awards for best global bank in Africa, African bank of the year, and banker of the year (African Business, 2008b). This reputational capital will no doubt help Nigerian banks to speed up their drive towards more M&As throughout Africa.

Nigerian bank presence abroad assumes different forms. They range from the establishment of full-fledged subsidiaries to the establishment of bank branches or representative offices. Nigerian banks have also been acquiring large shares in a number of African banks outside Nigeria. So far, the expansion strategy of Nigerian banks in Africa has been carried out in three stages. First, the banks focused on English-speaking countries close to home in West Africa. As a result, Nigerian banks have a strong presence in countries such as Ghana, Sierra Leone, Liberia and the Gambia. In the second stage, Nigerian banks strengthened their presence in the French-speaking part of West Africa, notably with the presence of several banks in Côte d'Ivoire, Benin and Burkina Faso. Third, Nigerian banks have recently been venturing outside their region to establish presence in a much broader set of African countries. These countries include Burundi, Cameroon, Rwanda, the Democratic Republic of the Congo, Zambia, Uganda, and even South Africa.

The expansion of the Nigerian banks is in large part due to a combination of two factors. First, the consolidation of Nigerian banks has created strong and viable financial institutions operating in the second-largest economy in sub-Saharan Africa. Second, there has been a change in the external environment faced by banks in recent years. While there used to be widespread protection of domestic financial markets and mistrust of foreign operators, it is now much easier to invest and operate across borders among African countries. Today, there is a more widespread acceptance of the idea that countries can benefit from more open financial services and higher competition. Particularly when entrants are experienced African banks, there is a feeling that they are more adapted to the specificities of the African market.

Another prominent West African investor in Africa's banking sector is Ecobank. This truly pan-African bank was created by ECOWAS and established in Lomé, Togo, in 1985, but the company was not licensed to operate as a bank until 1988. Through greenfield investments and M&As, Ecobank has pursued a proactive policy of African expansion and is now the leading pan-African banking group, present in more African countries than any other bank – 25 countries with over 500 branches. This is part of a dynamic strategy for geographical expansion that has resulted in this banking group being more widely present than any other on the continent, though it is only the 23rd by capital value (African Business, 2008b).

Its growth has occurred mainly in three separate phases. Ecobank started its operations in Togo in 1988 and quickly established presence in neighbouring Côte d'Ivoire and Nigeria in 1989, followed by Benin and Ghana in 1990. The next phase of expansion started in 1997 with branches in Burkina Faso and Mali. In 1999, Ecobank widened its presence in the West African region to Guinea, Liberia, Niger and Senegal. Between 2000 and 2005, Ecobank established presence in Cameroon and Cape Verde, but it is especially as of 2006 that the third wave of expansion began, when Ecobank started business in Sierra Leone and Chad. In 2007, Ecobank strengthened its presence in West Africa with new operations in Guinea Bissau, Sao Tome and Principe, and the Gambia. It also continued the expansion into Central Africa by opening subsidiaries in Cameroon, the Central African Republic and Rwanda. In 2008, this continued with Malawi, Congo, Kenya, Burundi, and the Democratic Republic of the Congo. Ecobank has plans to expand its presence in Africa to 33 countries this year, starting with Gabon, the United Republic of Tanzania and Zambia by mid-2009 (Ecobank, 2009).

Ecobank and Nigerian banks will affect intra-African investment in three major ways. First, whenever these banks open branches, merge with or acquire domestic banks, they inject capital in the economy and introduce new products and new managerial and technological skills. They also contribute to economic activity through their lending operations and savings mobilization. This alone contributes to the strengthening of the local financial sector. Second, due to more competition made possible by the coming of the new banks, the cost of banking services is going down in some countries (Nordas, 2001). Third, these banks have created financial networks across Africa, facilitating payment mechanisms between countries. The availability of cross-country payment mechanisms is one of the factors that will encourage intra-African trade and investment.

2. North African investment in Africa

Some North African countries have recently increased their investments in Africa. These investments occur not only between North African countries but also in countries south of the Sahara, especially in West Africa.

One of the countries whose presence in Africa has become more noticeable in recent years is the Libyan Arab Jamahiriya. In 2006, the country set up the Libyan Africa Portfolio for Investment (LAP), a sovereign wealth fund with over $5 billion in capital. This fund has become a dynamic force in Africa, investing in a wide range of sectors and in several African countries. One of its subsidiary companies, LAP Green Network, operates telecom companies in Uganda, Niger, Rwanda and Côte d'Ivoire. LAP also funds the Libya Arab Africa Investment Company, which invests in the sectors of telecom, mining, tourism, real estate, manufacturing and agriculture. It is present in 25 African countries spanning all regions of the continent.

The Libyan Arab Jamahiriya's neighbour Egypt has also been establishing a presence in Africa through investment, notably with the expansion of the Orascom business group. This large group, with a diverse portfolio of activities — including infrastructure development, construction, real estate and telecommunications — is present in several African countries. One of its principal companies, Orascom Telecom Holdings, is one of the largest and most diversified telecom operators in the world. Among other countries, it operates in Algeria, Tunisia and Zimbabwe. Another company in the group, Orascom Construction Industries, runs production units in Algeria and Nigeria.

As of 2000, Morocco has substantially deepened its economic ties with the rest of the African continent. An important signal in this new orientation was the decision by Morocco to cancel the debt of all African LDCs and grant them restriction-free access to the Moroccan market. In the following years, investments from Morocco to other African countries increased substantially, as an increasing number of Moroccan companies set up operations in the region. Moroccan mining companies are now present, for example, in Congo, Gabon, Guinea, Mali and Burkina Faso. Maroc Telecom, the national telecommunications company, has operations in Mauritania and Burkina Faso while Moroccan banks have established themselves in Tunisia and Algeria. Ynna Holdings, a Moroccan company active in construction and manufacturing, has operations in the Libyan Arab Jamahiriya, Tunisia, Egypt, Côte d'Ivoire, Mauritania, Gabon, Mali and Equatorial Guinea (Iraqi, 2007).

By far the most important destination of Moroccan investment in the region, however, is Senegal. Indeed, Moroccan companies active in Senegal include public transport companies such as the national shipping company COMANAV and the airline Royal Air Maroc, which have respectively taken over a passenger transport route and set up a new airline in partnership with the Government of Senegal. Private Moroccan companies are also strongly present in Senegal. Sectors in which they are active in Senegal include construction and public works, power, telecoms and the pharmaceutical industry (Iraqi, 2007). Since 2005, banks have also started to establish themselves strongly in the country, notably with the establishment of a subsidiary of Moroccan bank Attijariwafa, North Africa's largest bank (Wade, 2008).

3. South African investment in Africa

This section provides the main trends in the geographical destination and sector composition of South African intra-African investment flows. The analysis is based on data covering the period 2000–2007 from the Reserve Bank of South Africa.[34]

(a) Geographical distribution of South Africa's foreign investments

The distribution of intra-African investment according to inflows and outflows is divided into five main subregions: North Africa, West Africa, Central Africa, East Africa, and Southern Africa.[35] The overall stock of South Africa investment across the African continent is reported in Figure 5 which shows the balances of inflow and outflow at the end of each period. As used here, inflow represents the accumulated stock of inbound investment into South Africa from the rest of the continent whereas outflow represents South Africa's stock of accumulated outbound investment into the rest of the subregions.

The stock of investment between South Africa and other African countries has increased since 2000. In 2000, the stock of inbound capital exceeded that of outbound but since 2005, outbound has exceeded inbound. Furthermore, the gap between the inbound and outbound has increased. Figures 6 and 7 illustrate inflows and outflows, respectively, by sub regions. The flow of intra-African investment into South Africa shows the dominance of the Southern Africa region. In 2007, it accounted for about 70 per cent of total intra-African flows, implying that all the other regions, taken individually, have very small investments into South Africa.

The dominance of Southern Africa in the composition of intra-African investment into South Africa is not surprising. South African neighbouring countries benefit from South Africa's sophisticated economy, particularly its

Figure 5

South Africa's aggregate intra-African investment flows, 1999–2007

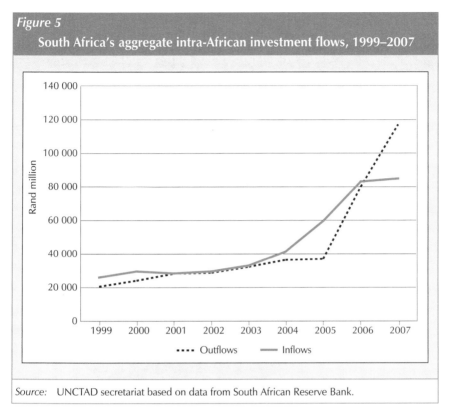

Source: UNCTAD secretariat based on data from South African Reserve Bank.

financial sector. Moreover, the close integration of South Africa into the sub-regional economy facilitates these resource transfers.

With respect to South African investments to other parts of Africa, figure 7 shows a more diversified distribution of investment outflows relative to inflows. East Africa and West Africa take the lion's share, with Southern Africa region as the third recipient of South African investments. This shows an asymmetry in the relationship between Southern Africa countries and South Africa. While the former consider South Africa as their key investment destination, South Africa has better investment opportunities in other regions. In fact, comparing the situation in 2007 to that in 2000 and 2004, the picture that seems to emerge is that South Africa's intra-African investment is shifting from Southern to West Africa. This could be a catch-up effect considering that South Africa's investment flows to West Africa are relatively recent in comparison to Southern Africa region.

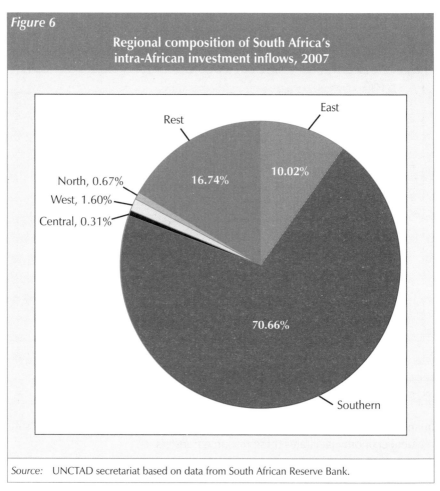

Figure 6

Regional composition of South Africa's intra-African investment inflows, 2007

Source: UNCTAD secretariat based on data from South African Reserve Bank.

Based on the observed pattern of movement in investment as described above, it is useful to identify sender and recipient countries in each region. Mauritius is the top actor in East Africa in both investment directions whereas in Southern Africa, Namibia and Mozambique rank at the top for outflow and inflow respectively. In West Africa, Nigeria is the most favoured country for both investing and more importantly, receiving investment.

(b) Composition of South Africa's foreign investment

The composition of foreign investment is made up of Foreign Direct Investment (FDI), Portfolio Investment and Other Investments. Other investment

Figure 7

Regional composition of South Africa's intra-African investment outflows, 2007

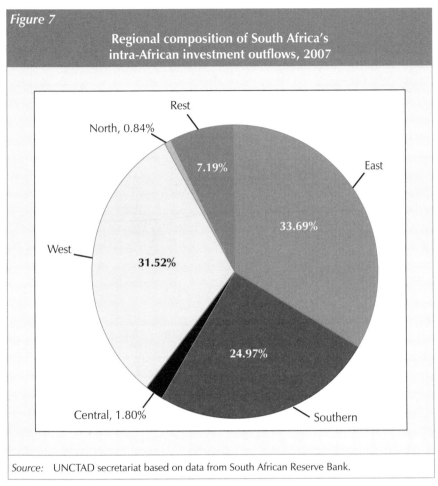

Source: UNCTAD secretariat based on data from South African Reserve Bank.

consists of loans, trade credits, deposits and other liabilities/assets. The analysis begins with an examination of the overall inflows and outflows and then shifts to composition of flows by sub regional destination. Figure 8 shows South Africa's investment decomposed into the three working categories defined above.

In the two figures, FDI and Portfolio flows are in opposite positions, with each ranking top in one aspect and lowest in the other correspondingly. It would, therefore, appear that portfolio investment into South Africa is financing FDI outflows from South Africa to the rest of the region. In effect, South Africa is trading financial assets for real assets in favor of the rest of the region thus using its relatively sophisticated financial markets to attract financial resources that are

Figure 8

Composition of South African intra-African investment, 1999–2007

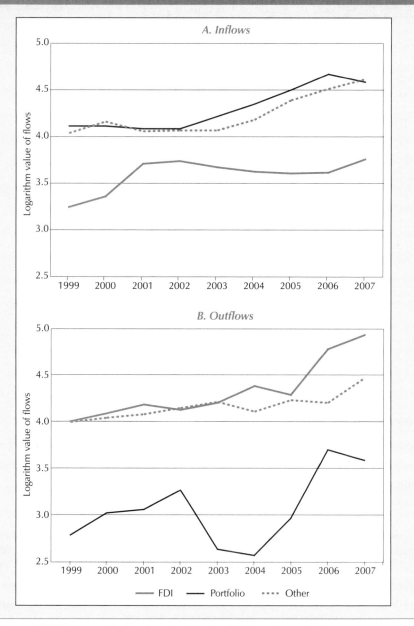

Source: UNCTAD secretariat based on data from South African Reserve Bank.

in turn invested across Africa. Simply stated, South Africa is promoting regional development financing and economic development through efficient financial intermediation.

There is a shift in emphasis from Southern Africa to West Africa as the main destination of FDI and differentiating FDI and portfolio investments helps to identify which components is driving the shift (figure 9).

Clearly, FDI is the dominant investment into West Africa, increasing from approximately 2.5 billion rand in 2000 to 34.8 billion rand in 2007.[36] Although outward investment into Southern Africa did not decrease, it nonetheless pales in comparison to the significant increase in FDI flow to West Africa. The subregional share for West Africa increased from 10.35 per cent in 2000 to 31.52 per cent in 2007, as shown in figures 9 and 10. Of the three countries accounting for South African investment in West Africa — Nigeria, Liberia and Ghana — the value of Nigeria's FDI share skyrocketed from 6 million rand (initially from the banking sector) to 31.7 billion rand in 2007 (private sector and banking). The increase in FDI flows between 2006 and 2007 was so spectacular that it will be difficult to sustain it.

Sector analysis of South Africa's foreign investment

Based on the categorization given by South Africa Reserve Bank, sector analysis is classified into monetary authority, public authorities, banks, private sector and public corporations. Figure 10 gives the flows of South Africa investment based on these sectors. The private sector is the dominant contributor to both outflow and inflow of South Africa's foreign investment. Furthermore, the growth of private foreign investment is higher than other sectors. The banking sector investment into South Africa also shows significant growth, in contrast to other sectors where the inflows have remained relatively constant over the years.

Because the private sector is the dominant driver of South Africa's foreign investment in both inflow and outflow, the regional analysis based on this particular sector is reported in table 13. Again, West Africa is the dominant destination, and over the years most of Africa's investment into South Africa has originated from West Africa as well. West Africa's share of inflow exceeds 80 per cent, followed by East Africa at slightly over 10 per cent.

Figure 9

Regional distribution of South Africa's FDI and portfolio investment, 1999–2007

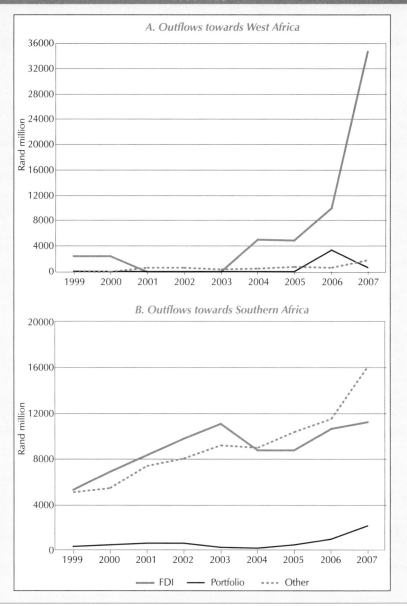

Source: UNCTAD secretariat based on data from South African Reserve Bank.

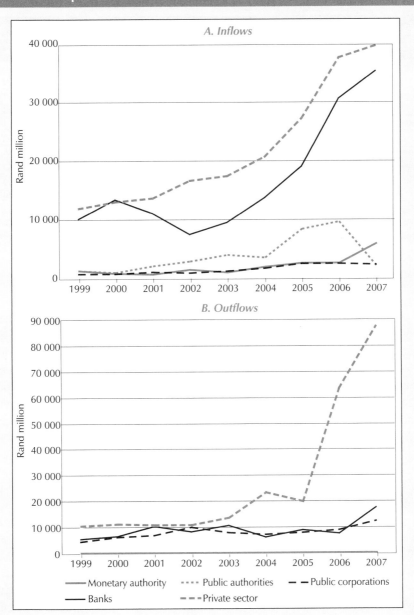

Figure 10

Sectoral composition of South Africa's intra-African investment, 1999–2007

Table 13

Value and share of South Africa private sector regional investment
(Rand millions)

Region	Private sector inflows (origin)			Private sector outflows (destination)		
	2000	*2004*	*2007*	*2000*	*2004*	*2007*
Central Africa	17 (0.12)	2 (0.01)	57 (0.14)	40 (0.36)	30 (0.13)	1 260 (1.43)
East Africa	1 864 (13.70)	2 615 (12.63)	5 194 (13.11)	2 604 (23.26)	8 595 (37.11)	37 442 (45.52)
West Africa	11 134 (81.86)	17 863 (86.27)	33 300 (84.05)	5 752 (51.39)	8 107 (35.00)	13 496 (15.32)
Southern Africa	20 (0.15)	170 (0.82)	190 (0.48)	2 472 (22.09)	5 303 (22.90)	33 379 (37.90)
North Africa	32 (0.24)	8 (0.04)	57 (0.14)	8 (0.07)	4 (0.02)	859 (0.98)
Rest of Africa	535 (3.93)	47 (0.23)	823 (2.08)	317 (2.83)	1 121 (4.84)	1 631 (1.85)
Total	**13 602**	**20 705**	**39 621**	**11 193**	**23 160**	**88 067**

Source: UNCTAD secretariat based on data from South African Reserve Bank.
Note: Number in parenthesis refers to the corresponding percentage value in that year.

Investment outflows tell a different comparative story which suggests a changing status regarding West Africa. In 2000, 51.39 per cent of South Africa's private foreign investment went into West Africa, followed by East Africa (23.26 per cent) and Southern Africa (22.09 per cent). However, in 2004, East Africa received 37.11 per cent, thus surpassing West Africa (35.00 per cent) to become the top destination, while Southern Africa remained unchanged at 22.90 per cent. In 2007, the pattern changed again with both East Africa (42.52 per cent) and Southern Africa (37.90 per cent) becoming the main destinations for South Africa's private foreign investment and West Africa's share decreasing to 15.32 per cent.

The key message from this table is that West Africa is the main source of regional private investment flow into South Africa in 2000 and 2007, whereas South Africa's private sector investment into West Africa was not as dominant. Instead, East Africa and Southern Africa were the main subregions hosting South African investment during this period.

In addition to analyzing the private sector dimension of South Africa's investment, the banking sector is reported in table 14.[37] West Africa is the main

Table 14
Distribution of South Africa's banking sector regional investment
(Rand millions)

Region	Banking sector inflows (origin)			Banking sector outflows (destination)		
	2000	*2004*	*2007*	*2000*	*2004*	*2007*
Central Africa	13 (0.10)	13 (0.09)	211 (0.59)	59 (0.88)	14 (0.23)	863 (4.88)
East Africa	3 094 (23.00)	735 (5.29)	2 646 (7.38)	4 794 (71.40)	2 306 (37.74)	1 848 (10.45)
West Africa	9 628 (71.57)	11 875 (85.42)	19 131 (53.37)	1 011 (15.06)	2 970 (48.60)	7 955 (44.99)
Southern Africa	21 (0.16)	283 (2.04)	1 181 (3.29)	29 (0.43)	343 (5.61)	1 649 (9.33)
North Africa	267 (1.98)	123 (0.88)	345 (0.96)	0 (0.00)	1 (0.02)	132 (0.75)
Rest of Africa	430 (3.20)	873 (6.28)	12 333 (34.40)	821 (12.23)	477 (7.81)	5 233 (29.60)
Total	13 453	13 902	35 847	6 714	6 111	17 680

Source: UNCTAD secretariat based on data from South African Reserve Bank.
Note: Number in parenthesis refers to the corresponding percentage value in that year.

source of regional investment in the banking sector. This finding is similar to that for the private sector. To summarize, the inflow of regional investment has been mainly from the private and the banking sectors. Recently, private sector flows have gone mainly to the East and Southern Africa subregions, while the banking sector has mainly been directed to West Africa.

A multidimensional view of the flow by type and sector reveals some interesting facts. First, the inflow of FDI over the years has come exclusively from the private sector, particularly Mauritius (East Africa). Similarly, the outflow of portfolio investment from South Africa has been mainly to West Africa (Ghana most recently). Furthermore, the outflow of FDI and inflow of portfolio are scrutinized because these two categories dominate the outflow and inflow of South Africa's investment. The private sector dominates in both FDI inflows and portfolio outflows. The banking sector has also invested increasingly until 2006. From tables 9 and 10, it is clear that South Africa is the favoured country for West African (Ghana, Liberia and Nigeria) private sector direct investment. On the other hand, East Africa and Southern Africa is the subregion for South Africa's private sector portfolio investment.

C. Conclusion

Intra-African FDI is estimated at 13 per cent of total foreign investment flows to Africa. This share is small, particularly relative to that in other developing regions such as South-East Asia, where intraregional investment represents 30 per cent of the total. Given the general need for more investment in Africa, intra-African investment should play a bigger role. Examples from West Africa and South Africa highlight the potential for increasing intra-African investment. Having a sound financial sector appears to be a prerequisite for increasing the flows of investment within Africa.

Chapter 4

EMERGING ISSUES IN REGIONAL TRADE INTEGRATION IN AFRICA: SERVICES, LABOUR MOBILITY AND MIGRATION

This chapter discusses services trade — in particular trade facilitation and logistics services — and labour mobility and migration. While it is recognized that these subjects have been elaborated on and discussed in the regional context, they are considered emerging issues because, unlike other areas of regional integration — e.g. goods — they are still in their early phases of development. The succeeding sections will highlight the importance of the contribution of these areas of cooperation to a successful regional integration process in Africa.

A. Services trade, trade facilitation and logistics services

1. Why intra-African services matters

(a) General considerations

A remarkable feature of the recent wave of regional trade agreements (RTAs) is the inclusion of provisions on trade in services in many such agreements.[38] This development could be attributed to a number of factors, including (a) the lowering of tariffs, which prompted policymakers to turn their attention to other barriers restricting international commerce (services appears to be one of the sectors characterized by numerous restrictions); (b) the growth of world goods trade and the emergence of international production networks, which have highlighted the importance of having an efficient services infrastructure such as telecommunications, finance, logistics or professional services; (c) market opening in services, which offers the prospect of performance improvements in services. Goods producers can draw on multinational service networks in organizing their business (Fink and Jansen, 2007).

Services represent, or have the potential to become, significant sources of export earnings for a large number of African economies. This is particularly true of sectors such as tourism, trade logistic services (transport, harbours, etc.)

or construction, among others. For example, Kenya, South Africa and other countries in the region are major tourist destinations, and Benin, Côte d'Ivoire, Kenya, Senegal and the United Republic of Tanzania earn substantial fees from the imports and exports of neighbouring landlocked countries transiting through their harbours.

In addition, because many services — such as telecommunications, banking, insurance, professional or transport services (so-called producer services) — are inputs to other economic activities, they can either facilitate or hinder trade and production in other economic sectors, both goods and services, depending on the efficiency with which they are made available to users. Currently, because of either the absence/lack of or poor quality of many services, especially producer services, most African countries either are unable to provide domestically the quantity or quality of producer services demanded by local producers and exporters, thus undermining their competitiveness, or are forced to import a substantial amount of such services, thereby exacerbating balance-of-payments difficulties. These point to the importance of an efficient services sector on trade efficiency, a favourable trade balance of most African countries, and the competitiveness of African producers, both domestic and international.

The above considerations help explain the growing recognition by African governments that the development of a healthy services sector is critical to the development of their economies. Yet, the development of service industries may require financial, human and technological resources that are not available locally – neither from the public or private sector. This may be the case because markets are too small and financial and human resources are too restricted. Also, monopolistic situations that prevailed in the past have made current operators complacent and unimaginative. In line with this observation, there is a growing understanding that regional integration could be a critical element to take into consideration, as policymakers turn their attention to forging new policies for the development of services. Furthermore, regional services trade offers a supportive environment for national firms by accelerating learning curves, building supply capacities and enhancing international competitiveness. Regional services trade also plays a catalytic role in generating employment and furthering the development of growing regional services industries and firms. By allowing for economies of scale in the production of services, RTAs may support the development of regional infrastructure in key sectors such as transportation, communications and energy (UNCTAD, 2007c).

(b) The particular importance of trade facilitation

Trade facilitation and efficient transport and logistics services have emerged in recent years as key determinants for successful market access. The quality of trade logistics and trade-related information flows has a direct bearing on regional trade dynamics, with possible attendant effects on structural changes and growth. Without adequate attention given to improving trade logistics, a strong regional dynamic is unlikely to unfold. The concrete forms of cooperation in this area will have to be adapted to the specific needs, institutional capacity and culture of cooperation in each region. Globally fragmented production processes and just-in-time inventory techniques have made speed, transparency, and security essential for integration into global value chains.

International trade and transportation take place within a complex administrative and operational environment. Trade facilitation attempts to achieve a more predictable, secure and cost-efficient trading environment through the simplification, standardization and harmonization of trade and transport procedures, and documents and information flows associated with a cross-border trade.

Trade facilitation is of particular relevance in the African development context. African intraregional trade and imports from and exports into Africa are confronted with excessive transaction costs, uncertainty and delays. Sub-Saharan African countries face comparatively longer time-frames to import, and exports have higher transport costs as well as a relatively high number of documentation requirements. Such barriers to trade impact trade flows and even offset gains from trade openness through tariff liberalization. Of the 118 countries monitored by the World Economic Forum (WEF) Global Enabling Trade Index, only 2 of 17 sub-Saharan African countries are amongst the middle-performing countries — Mauritius (40th) and South Africa (59th).

With such high barriers to trade, regional economic integration also lags behind and its potential is hampered. Operational and administrative barriers to intraregional trade have to be removed to fully realize the benefits of a single market, free trade area or customs union. Furthermore, trade facilitation solutions are more effective when implemented across countries — on a regional or at least bilateral level through cooperation and harmonization. The regional dimension of trade facilitation is likely to grow in importance the more countries strive to implement trade and transport facilitation reforms. Although largely based on global standards, efficient trade facilitation reform has to be applied in a regionally coordinated manner. For example, joint development of applications and sharing of infrastructure and development of regional standards are the most efficient way to harmonize procedures and formalities and reduce the cost of doing business substantially. Countries can also benefit from each other through sharing of best practices and enhancing capacity-building activities.

(c) The particular challenges of landlocked countries

Of the world's 31 landlocked developing countries (LLDCs), 15 are located in Africa. Transit dependence normally increases transaction costs and reduces competitiveness. The main problems for LLDCs are frequently the geographical remoteness and the dependence on trade and transport systems in neighbouring and/or coastal countries.

LLDCs' particular geographic disadvantage explains to a large degree the difficulty of trading with them — both logistics-wise and cost-wise. UNCTAD statistics shows that estimated freight costs of imports to African LLDCs are three to five times higher than the world average estimated freight costs for imports (UNCTAD, 2008e). A recent World Bank study, "Transport prices and costs in Africa", highlights the fact that considerable costs are incurred in relation to delays for both picking up cargo at ports and crossing borders. Delays both in ports and at borders vary from an average of 5 hours to more than 30 hours in the worst cases. Aside from the geographic disadvantage, other reasons for higher costs of trading with LLDCs are unreliable import and export chains due to inadequate transit procedures, overregulation, multiple controls and poor service.

Given these, it is even more pressing to foster regional initiatives in the area of trade facilitation, particularly those that would benefit landlocked countries in the African region. It is already a well-known fact that Benin, Côte d'Ivoire, Kenya, Senegal and the United Republic of Tanzania earn substantial fees from the imports and exports of neighbouring landlocked countries transiting through their harbours. Thus, there is an incentive for these countries also to invest in linking LLDCs to key harbours, as facilitating trade would improve the economies of these LLDCs. These neighboring countries themselves could also benefit from an improved economic performance of these LLDCs, as the latter attract more trade passing through these transit countries.

2. How regional integration agreements consider services

Until recently, cooperation and integration in the area of services remained marginal in regional integration arrangements among African countries.

Most of the subregional and regional agreements deal with the mere facilitation of services among countries. Cooperation among member states is limited for the most part to measures geared at the coordination and harmonization of rules and regulations affecting service activities. For example, several regional or bilateral agreements deal with the facilitation of services among various modes of road and rail transport. ECOWAS has enacted decisions concerning the facilitation of transport services within the region, such as the decision relative to the harmonization of highway legislation, and decisions such as the creation of liability insurance for transit and transport operations. Other types of cooperation took the form of harmonization of mechanisms for the exchange of information and experiences, and initiatives promoting joint research and training programmes on services.

An equally significant number of these agreements facilitate the joint provision of services. This involves mostly infrastructure services. One example is the creation in 1985 within the Preferential Trade Area (PTA) for Eastern and Southern African States of the Bank for Trade and Development. Its mission is to secure financing for multinational projects and promote trade among the 19 member states. Finally, a more limited number of agreements deal with collaboration among corporations and other professional interests from the same sector of activity in several countries. This usually translates into the creation of sector-specific associations, e.g. bankers, restaurant owners, hotel keepers, journalists, etc. The creation by ECOWAS of Ecobank, a private offshore bank, is an example of transnational business collaboration.

The above three types of measures could be described as cooperation but not integration, which is oriented toward the creation of a wider economic space for service providers at the regional or subregional level, by means of mutual market opening and preferential treatment among member states. Integration thus implies progressive implementation of liberalization principles of transactions, non-discrimination and coordination of member states' policies and legislation. The AEC Treaty, the revised Treaty of ECOWAS and COMESA, and SADC have all introduced explicit provisions relating to national treatment, right of establishment, free movement of capital or free movement of labour.

These form the legal basis through which effective integration in services can be achieved.

Thus far, however, there is very limited progress in terms of the implementation of these integration provisions in RTAs. At best, what we observed are trade facilitation and sectoral cooperation in key services infrastructure, which will be discussed in the succeeding sections.

(a) Sectoral regional initiatives to foster cooperation and integration in trade facilitation, transport and logistics services

Subregional initiatives in this area encompass harmonization of procedures, adoption of cross-border insurance schemes, transit guarantee systems, documents, and the cooperation and information exchange amongst customs administration. As a result of reform efforts, ECOWAS member states now use a single customs document for importation, exportation, transit and other customs regimes. ECOWAS members also adopted the harmonized system as customs nomenclature and use a common certificate of origin. The WAEMU subregion currently undertakes a comprehensive project to set up joint border posts. Members are also reviving the Inter-State Road Transit Convention (TRIE). COMESA progressed in the area of cross-border transport facilitation through the adoption of the COMESA Carrier's License, COMESA motor vehicle third-party insurance scheme and the harmonization of road transit charges. In the customs area, COMESA members adopted the COMESA Customs Declaration Documents (COMESA-CD) and adopted the customs nomenclature. Members also plan to launch a regionally recognized Customs Bond Guarantee. SADC members adopted the common customs document SAD 500 for importation, exportation and transit custom regimes, but so far only South Africa has adopted it. On the subregional SACU level, members regulate cross-border traffic rights for the transportation of goods transit through the SACU cross-border transport permits.

These recent trade facilitation efforts are taking place against the backdrop of the ongoing negotiations on trade facilitation at WTO. With the negotiations, WTO members aim at clarifying and improving relevant aspects of General Agreement on Tariffs and Trade articles V, VIII; and X (respectively freedom of transit, fees and formalities, and publication and administration of trade regulations).

Numerous proposals on trade facilitation provisions have been put forward by delegations. They include trade-related information, expediting clearance and release of goods, strengthening uniform administration of trade regulations, simplification and reduction of procedures and formalities, strengthening of transit guarantee systems, and national and cross-border border agency coordination. Many of those proposed provisions have a regional dimension for implementation. Hence, to the extent that regional trade facilitation objectives are in line with the negotiated commitments at WTO, the multilateral negotiation process can contribute to advancing regional reforms — in particular, if technical assistance for the implementation is forthcoming.

(b) Other sectoral regional initiatives

In accordance to various legal provisions contained in the treaties of African regional economic communities, member states have taken some regional sectoral initiatives with the objective of promoting those specific sectors. This section will highlight the objectives of these initiatives.

Tourism

In order to maximize the COMESA region's revenue earning from tourism, COMESA has defined a regional tourism strategy. The major elements of this strategy include a system for licensing, standardization of hotel classification and harmonization of the professional standards of agents in the tourism and travel industry within COMESA. The regional tourism policy also aims to promote joint ventures between local and foreign entrepreneurs. Furthermore, the composite nature of tourism makes the establishment of formal links with other sectors such as transport and communications, whose inputs the industry requires for a complete tourism product, all the more necessary.[39] The COMESA investment promotion agencies aim to promote investment opportunities e.g. within the areas of tourism and infrastructure, while enhancing intra-COMESA investment and trade within the COMESA member states.

Another similar regional tourism initiative is found in SADC. The Regional Tourism Organization of Southern Africa is responsible for promoting and marketing tourism in this region. As such, it has taken various initiatives such as running road shows, organizing seminars on tourism development and supporting tourism promotion of all 14 member countries.

Because of the economic importance and the rapid expansion of the tourism sector in the COMESA and EAC regions, the two regional economic integration arrangements are addressing jointly a number of challenges affecting this sector. Among these challenges, are improving of existing infrastructure and facilities, developing air connections both inter-COMESA and to target markets, increasing market awareness of the regional product and diversity offerings, implementing environmental best practice, and increasing regional investments.

Communications

An interesting example of private sector-driven regional integration is found in the telecommunications industry. Realizing that roaming interconnectivity was crucial for many African subscribers whose family, social and business communities transgressed political borders, MTC and Celtel launched in 2006 its "One Network" borderless network for East Africa. One Network enabled its subscribers in Kenya, Uganda and the United Republic of Tanzania to use their subscriptions in any of those countries to make calls at local rates without roaming surcharges, as well as to receive incoming calls free of charge and recharge their prepaid accounts with any of the local top-up cards. In June 2007, One Network was being extended to six more African countries, the plan being to ultimately provide a seamless network in all 15 African countries of operation. MTC and Celtel, before and after the acquisition, are examples of successful private sector investment and operation in the mobile telephony sector in developing countries (UNCTAD, 2008d).

3. Suggestions for a possible positive agenda for regional cooperation and integration

In spite of the multiplicity of regional agreements, there remain numerous barriers to trade, and national reports generally underline the low impact that these agreements have had so far. However, the experiences highlighted above showed successful experiences on cooperation in certain services sectors aimed at better facilitating trade in services. The harmonization of freight rates within the framework of PTA, the removal of obstacles to the free movement of persons and of capital among ECOWAS countries constitute initiatives that reflect the will to eliminate obstacles to regional trade, including trade in services.

However, a number of obstacles to full economic integration remain, including (a) the existence of political barriers for the implementation of regional integration obligations (which remains primarily the obligation of national leaders); (b) internal weakness and inefficiencies of national economies, including infrastructural weaknesses, a non-existent or weak private sector and deficiencies in the regulatory system of countries; (c) conceptual inadequacies in some cooperation agreements, including the absence in some earlier treaties of provisions that are relevant for the integration of services, such as the free movement of capital and labour, right of establishment, national treatment and the necessary mechanisms to ensure conformity with member states; and (d) the general lack of interest among the expected key players to move forward in the framework of regional entities, especially as they are able to pursue their economic interests with key partners at the bilateral level and in other areas of relationships, e.g. AGOA, and other preferential arrangements that they currently benefit from.

Yet, the fact that there are very positive experiences of cooperation among African countries in trade facilitation involving key infrastructure services is a recognition of the advantages that such cooperation brings to regional partners in terms of efficiency, competitiveness and ease of doing business.

Given this, it is imperative to build on the different forms of cooperation that now exist, with the aim of moving towards full integration. As countries are at different levels of economic, regulatory, institutional and infrastructural preparedness, among others, a gradual, phased-in participation is encouraged, with varying sets of obligations for different countries, but with the explicit understanding that progressively, each of the partners would be subjected to the same rules and expectations. In the Asian region, for example, the Association of South-east Asian Nations (ASEAN) has implemented a gradual approach in the integration of new members, phasing in compliance to certain obligations, thus the practice of ASEAN minus (i.e. ASEAN minus the new members or some of them).

Politically, it is imperative to have leaders think beyond the short-term gains and consider the long-term benefits of cooperation in enhancing the economic performances of the region as a whole and broaden their markets. Better trade facilitation and more harmonized rules and administrative procedures would attract more trade into the region. This would result in more diversified partnerships, including both Northern and Southern partners, in order to reduce the vulnerability of the continent to shocks or downfalls in the North, as for instance, the economic and financial crisis that the world is experiencing now.

Likewise, there are positive spillover effects of economic growth and stability in the partner countries and regions on their respective security and political stability, making the region more attractive to other partners, both Northern and Southern.

In addition, cooperation in the key infrastructure services would likewise facilitate the venturing of bigger and more stable players in the region into greenfield investments in many of the less developed African countries. They should take advantage of their geographical and cultural affinities to strengthen their regional linkages, and the area of services could be one such opportunity.

Finally, African leaders should take advantage of the developments at WTO, in particular the discussions on trade facilitation. Many proposals have regional dimensions to the extent that regional trade facilitation objectives are in line with the negotiated commitments at WTO, the multilateral negotiation process can contribute to advancing regional reforms — in particular, if technical assistance for the implementation is forthcoming. It is to be noted that one of the objectives of the WTO negotiations is to provide trade facilitation-related technical assistance. Delegations in these negotiations have attempted to design special and differential treatment provisions that link the application of commitments to countries' individual implementation capacity, and technical assistance delivery for capacity acquisition.

B. Labour mobility and migration

1. Why facilitating intra-African migration is important for the continent's development

Migration, in the most general sense, covers all types of movement of people for varying reasons and durations of stay. Migration could be internal, i.e. movements within a given country, or international, i.e. movement of citizens of country A to country B.[40] Thus, labour-related migration, or labour mobility, is just one subset of migration. Aside from labour mobility, borrowing from the trade jargon, the term free movement of people has been coined to also refer to labour mobility. Most free trade agreements and other regional trade agreements refer to their provision on labour mobility as free movement of people, notably, agreements that came after WTO had adopted the General Agreement on Trade in Services (GATS). [41]

In this section, the terms labour mobility and free movement of persons/ people refer to international migration in search of economic opportunities. While it is recognized that there are some nuances between these concepts, it is beyond this paper to elaborate on those. As the different regional economic cooperation arrangements and the other regional forums and mechanisms use any one or a combination of these terms, the paper will refer to the terms as used by these regional groups/forums. It is to be noted, however, that migration is the broadest of the three terms, as it encompasses the whole range of aspects relating to such movements, including the socio-cultural and the developmental aspects that accompany international migration, which this section will tackle.

In an increasingly integrated world, international migration is bound to continue and will likely expand. This is particularly true in the African region, where movements of people have been commonplace, particularly among contiguous states and countries within the subregion. Recognizing the importance of the free movement of people, the Abuja Treaty of June 1991 establishing the African Economic Community (AEC), urged member states to adopt employment policies that allow the free movement of persons within the community. This entailed the strengthening and establishment of labour exchanges aimed at facilitating the employment of available skilled manpower of one member state in other member states (article 71 (e)) as an essential component for the promotion of regional cooperation and integration in Africa. African governments, recognizing the complexity of international migration, are working out through the AU a pan-African migration strategy that is comprehensive and would ensure the maximum benefits of migration to sending countries. Through this overall thrust, and coupled with developments in the context of NEPAD and the African Economic Community, enhancing intra-African migration, if it is well managed, can enhance cooperation in other areas, notably trade and investment, in the various regional economic communities (RECs).

Facilitating labour mobility and migration would result in a win–win situation for all actors concerned. Specifically, for home or origin countries, migration brings remittances, facilitates the creation of business and trade networks, as well as the transfer of skills and technology, among others. For receiving countries, migrants fill in the required human resource and skill gap in key sectors of the economy as well as the social system (e.g. health workers). Costs identified for origin countries relate mainly to brain drain and issues of abuse of migrants and other social concerns (e.g. erosion of the family), while for receiving countries, there are concerns that migrants compete with locals for employment, wage effects and other concerns relating to social and cultural integration, security, and social and health infrastructure.

While there are tendencies for destination countries to restrict the free movement of labour, there is evidence of these countries' benefiting tremendously from migrants' presence in their economies. In West Africa, for example, it is now widely accepted that the "Ivorian miracle" of the 1980s is attributable to the inflow of Sahelian labour on cocoa and coffee plantations in the South of Côte d'Ivoire. Lesotho, Swaziland, Mozambique and Malawi have all been instrumental in meeting South Africa's labour requirements, in particular in the mining, agricultural and domestic services sectors.

For sending countries, migrants' remittances form a large part of these countries' GDPs, as in the case of Lesotho, where remittances, mainly from workers in South Africa, constitute close to 25 per cent of its GDP. More significantly, remittances have contributed to the upkeep of the migrants' families back home, with positive implications on education and health outcomes.

Given the reality of migration and the movement of labour within the African region and the recognition of African leaders themselves of the importance of addressing this issue at the regional level, it is imperative to build on the existing initiatives on facilitating labour mobility and migration management already laid out in various RECs and other consultative forums in the region. Such existing mechanisms leading to a cooperative exchange of skills could be used to rationalize a holistic pan-African labour mobility arrangement. This arrangement would not only serve to meet the specific labour needs of destination countries at a given time, but also boost the qualifications and competencies of African labour and elevate it to international renown. This African pool of "talents" would likewise serve as attractions for the entry of foreign investments, including outsourced services.

2. How regional integration agreements treat labour mobility and migration trade

At the regional level, there is a clear recognition that labour mobility and migration management should form part of the Pan-African integration schemes. Commencing with the adoption of the Abuja Treaty in 1991 — which urged, among other things, that member countries adopt employment policies that allow the free the free movement of people in Africa — succeeding OAU summit-

---

Box 3. Dynamics of intra-African migration

Overwhelming share of intra-African migration:

As explained earlier in this chapter, African migrants mostly remain in the continent (some 69 per cent). However, emigrants from the North African subregion, many of them sub-Saharan migrants in transit, tend to move beyond the continent. The United Nations estimated that there were 191 million migrants in 2005, of which 17 million were widely distributed in the African continent (or 1.9 per cent of the African population). Historically, large Western and Southern African countries have hosted a dominant share of migrants. The top five African countries with the largest immigrants in 2005 were Côte d'Ivoire (2.4 million), Ghana (1.7 million), South Africa (1.1 million), Nigeria (1.0 million) and the United Republic of Tanzania (0.8 million), collectively accepting 40 per cent of migrants in Africa. The top five African countries/areas with the largest immigrants relative to population in 2005 were Gabon (17.7 per cent), Gambia (15.3 per cent), Côte d'Ivoire (13.1 per cent), and the Libyan Arab Jamahiriya (10.6 per cent).

Large share of extra-African remittances:

According to World Bank estimates for 2007, Africa countries received 6.8 per cent of total global remittances of $337 billion, i.e. $23.1 billion. Individually, North African countries received relatively more remittances than sub-Saharan African countries. For 2005, the flows to individual North African countries (much from outside of the African continent) were estimated to be at $11.4 billion, compared to $11.7 billion shared among sub-Saharan African countries. However, the size of remittances relative to GDP in African is relatively small, although there are some striking exceptions, such as Lesotho (28 per cent of GDP).

Source: United Nations Population Division, World Bank.

level discussions dealt with issues relating to migration, including strengthening intergovernmental cooperation. In June 2000, the OAU Council of Ministers adopted a Strategic Framework for Policy on Migration in Africa, which provided member states with concrete policy guidelines on various migration-related subjects. In 2006, the AU Executive Council adopted the African Common Position on Migration and Development, which highlighted, among others, the need "to ensure coordination in the development of common regional policies for the management of migration within the RECs".

Many African policymakers have argued for greater labour mobility, citing restricted movement of factors of production, especially labour, across national boundaries as a major constraint to regional integration in Africa (ECA, 2006a). Existing regional economic cooperation schemes contain provisions on free movement of persons as well as right of residence and establishment.

ECOWAS adopted a new treaty in 2003 recognizing the right of free movement of community citizens and the right to work in member countries. As of 2006, however, only the entitlement to travel without visa for up to 90 days had been implemented.

Citizens of the EAC can now obtain an EAC passport, together with, among others, a single immigration entry/departure card under more harmonized procedures of issuances of entry/work permits. EAC citizens are now entitled to visa-free entry in member countries, which has reduced administrative burdens facing some migrants (Shaw, 2007). A common EAC passport, valid only within the community, entitles the holder to an automatic six-month multiple visa for travel to any EAC member country. Reportedly, there are plans to upgrade the passport for use beyond EAC borders (ECA, 2006b).

After the withdraw in 1997 of its initial protocol by the Governments of South Africa, Namibia and Botswana, SADC adopted a new protocol at the 2005 summit. It provides for visa-free entry for up to 90 days per year of nationals from member countries. The protocol also authorizes permanent and temporary residence as well as working in the territory of another member country. Nevertheless, the protocol still needs to be ratified by at least by nine (i.e. two thirds) of the SADC member states.

In 2001, member states of COMESA adopted a protocol on the free movement of persons, labour, services, rights of establishment and right of residence. However, progress in terms of concrete implementation of the protocol has been slow. For the time being, COMESA member countries continue with a provisional protocol on the gradual relaxation and eventual elimination of visa requirement within the PTA treaty.

While labour mobility is included in the protocol and objectives of several African regional economic communities, many practical obstacles still hamper its effective realization. As a result, labour markets remain fragmented, serving as a barrier to the free movement of labour among countries (ECA, 2006a: 17). Overall, the African regional organizations have taken steps to facilitate short-term stays in member countries, but the establishment of large economic unions within which citizens could move and work freely remains a longer-term goal.

During the last decade or so, various regional consultative processes (RCPs) have emerged to complement the efforts of formal regional integration arrangements to facilitate the movement of people. More than just facilitating mobility of workers, RCPs cover a wider range of migration management concerns and bring together a broader set of actors including government representatives, representatives of regional grouping, international organizations and, in some cases, civil society organizations. The focus of RCPs is on cooperative dialogue and on seeking common understanding on migration issues. Goals are identified and, often, non-binding recommendations or plans of action are adopted (United Nations, 2004).

In Africa, three RCPs have been established. The Migration Dialogue for Southern African (MIDSA) was formally established in 2000 for SADC member countries. The MIDSA has since periodically held consultations, thereby exploring ways of improving the management of border control and labour migration by means of technical cooperation, training and information-sharing among governments (International Organization for Migration (IOM), 2005). The Migration Dialogue for Western Africa (MIDWA) was established in 2002 as a follow-up process to the Dakar Declaration adopted in 2000 at the West Africa Regional Ministerial Meeting on the Participation of Migrants in the Development of their Country of Origin. The MIDWA seeks regional approaches to combating trafficking in persons, to addressing issues linked to labour migration, and to promoting peace and stability in Western Africa (IOM, 2005). In May 2008, the-Inter-Governmental Authority on Development — Regional Consultative Process on Migration (IGAD-RCP) was launched as the mechanism for continuous dialogue and cooperation among six Eastern African countries: Djibouti, Ethiopia, Kenya, Somalia, Sudan and Uganda.

Pragmatism tends to dictate RCPs which can provide the common interest of participants. They are well positioned to add coherence to the broader regional agenda and complement formal regional processes by involving neighbouring or like-minded states in special or ad hoc discussions. Similarly, they are well placed to enhance bilateral cooperation by creating trust between countries and generating opportunities for interaction in a broader setting (IOM, 2008). Nevertheless, the number of RCPs specializing in labour migration is still limited (IOM, 2008). Furthermore, owing to their non-binding nature, their impact on the development of national labour migration policies is difficult to assess. Indeed, the informality of these processes may be seen as a strength (as this fosters broader participation) and as a weakness (as the discretion of each country regarding the results of consultation remains firm).

3. Challenges facing intra-African migration and suggestions for a positive agenda for its development

Overall, free movement of people and/or labour mobility in Africa has been impeded by any or a combination of the following: economic contractions, xenophobic sentiments, political pressures to secure jobs for local workers, among others. It is, however, a reality that there are demands within the continent for workers, even on a seasonal basis, thus the need for well-managed migration.

While there have been various references to the need to achieve the objective of free movement of people, including in regional economic cooperation agreements, the provisions and protocols relating to free labour mobility have not been implemented. Thus, while all of the African RECs reviewed in the chapter contain provisions and protocols for the free movement of people and the right of residence and establishment, these rights have yet to be translated into national laws. This may also require amending national laws and investment codes that restrict "foreigners", including nationals of community states, from participating in certain kinds of economic activities. The regional push and initiatives towards harmonization at the regional level of laws and regulations on labour mobility should be sustained through political will. One could also think of phasing in implementation of agreements.

As to other avenues of facilitating movement of people, i.e. WTO and EPAs, these cover a very limited set of movements — specific categories of people moving to provide services on specific sectors. Moreover, current commitments at WTO offer very limited opportunities for African service providers to enter other WTO members' services market. Thus, these do not offer real alternatives to regional cooperation on labour mobility for African countries.

Migration's development impacts have been well-documented and, for African countries in particular, tapping the developmental contributions of migration (e.g. use of remittances in productive activities) could contribute to improving some of these countries' poverty levels and states of health and education. Thus, an African regional migration framework, either inside or outside the RECs, must take into account the inclusion of the development dimension of migration.

Labour mobility within the African region has been observed since time immemorial and has fueled the growth of the economies of some countries in the region. The Abuja Treaty of 1991 itself recognized the importance of the free movement of people and urged various regional economic initiatives to progressively allow for the free movement of persons within the region. While RECs contain provisions or protocols for free movement of people, they fall short of implementing these provisions owing to various economic, political and social-cultural reasons. The realities, however, point toward the need for greater mobility and thus the call for harmonization of laws and regulations on labour mobility, so as to better manage migration to maximize its development impacts. This will promote a truly positive agenda for intra-African migration/labour mobility needed for the continent to mitigate the adverse consequences of North–South brain drain while ensuring knowledge-driven cooperative exchange of skills among African countries. In the end, such an approach should be much more productive than the promotion of national defensive polices by individual countries.

Chapter 5

STRENGTHENING REGIONAL INTEGRATION IN AFRICA: SOME POLICY RECOMMENDATIONS

These recommendations are based on a strategic vision of the role of regional integration in the development process. African policymakers should consider regional integration as part of a broader development strategy. Integrating Africa's fragmented markets can help attract the required investments, from both Africa and the rest of the world, to build competitive and more diversified economies through better production systems that are more responsive to development objectives. Seen from this perspective, regional integration is expected to offer more economic opportunities in terms of investment, production, and trade and factor mobility. This, in turn, should strengthen African countries' integration into the global economy.

A. Intra-African trade in goods

Despite its relatively low level in aggregate terms, intra-African trade represents an important share of many African countries' total external trade. Moreover, the potential for increasing intra-African trade remains untapped. In order to exploit such potential, it is imperative to tackle the most binding constraints to intra-African trade. The following policy recommendations are indications of some of the measures African countries could consider taking to unlock the opportunities offered by regional economic integration.

1. Deepening regional economic integration to help rather than frustrate Africa's participation in the world economy

Regional integration should not be used to isolate Africa from the rest of the world economy. Instead, integration should be used as a building bloc for Africa's effective integration into the world economy. It is encouraging to note that the EPAs currently under negotiation across Africa seem to share this objective. Given the fragmented nature of current RTAs, their rationalization should be a policy priority before they could be used as relevant entities to help Africa's effective integration into the world economic system. In this regard, the announcement in late 2008 that COMESA, EAC and SADC planned to merge to form a free trade area is a welcome proposal. Landlocked countries, particularly, should be at the forefront of regional integration efforts given the benefits they stand to gain.

2. Adopting a regional cooperation strategy centred on infrastructure development

One of the reasons why the aggregate figure of intra-Africa trade remains very low is that countries have so far pursued a process of integration favouring institutional arrangements at the expense of physical integration. The bulky nature of intra-African trade requires efficient transport systems, which are now lacking. The importance of infrastructure for Africa's economic integration is well recognized. Some financing modalities have been set up to address the infrastructure constraint. Africa should take maximum advantage of opportunities for infrastructure finance, such as those under the Infrastructure Consortium for Africa (ICA).[42] In this light, regional infrastructure development should be part of the yardsticks used to assess progress with regional integration.

In addition, African countries need to address several domestic measures which are against the development of regional trade. Countries should undertake a thorough review of their trade sector, identify its weaknesses and adopt a strategy to put in place the right trade facilitation measures. For example, there are cases where trade can be speeded up through simplification of administrative procedures combined with some basic investment in trade facilitation technologies. Moreover, introducing competition in the transport sector can reduce transport costs considerably. The effect of these measures on easing trade can be remarkable, as some examples in Africa have shown. In Angola, modernization of customs has cut processing time dramatically (only 24 hours are needed now) and customs revenue has increased by 150 per cent. In Ghana, customs clearing time at the airport has been reduced from three days to four hours on average as a result of the adoption of a more efficient technology and simplification of procedures. Revenue from airport traffic has increased by 30 per cent. Similar reforms in Mozambique resulted in a 58 per cent increase in customs revenue. The return to investment in these efficiency-enhancing reforms is often very high. In Mozambique, it took only 14 months to recover the initial investment in trade facilitation through additional revenue generated by the reforms (Milner et al., 2008).

3. Adopting a clear development strategy to help Africa defend its interests

Trade policy should be part of an overall long-term development strategy which defines a country's development objectives and the way they should be reached. The lack of such a coherent framework in many African countries has prevented them from maximizing the benefits they could derive from bilateral and multilateral economic relations. Conceiving trade policy outside a development strategy could help explain why trade has not brought the expected development benefits to many countries in Africa (UNCTAD, 2008a). When a long-term development vision is in place, it is relatively easy to determine what role trade should play to achieve some of the development objectives. This strategy would also help Africa gain more from its engagement with the rest of the world.

At the regional level, the conception of a regional African development strategy could draw from the NEPAD spatial development programme. Launched in 2007, this programme identifies possible economic clusters in different regions as well as strategic activities that can support these clusters with specific milestones and outputs. The key goals are to (a) stimulate investment-led economic growth and development; (b) facilitate trade, including intra-Africa trade; (c) promote regional economic cooperation and integration; (d) optimize the utilization of infrastructure; (e) encourage economic diversification; (f) enhance the competitiveness of African economies; and (g) stimulate employment and wealth creation (NEPAD, 2006). Operationalizing this programme at the country level will require integrating it into individual African countries' own development strategies.

B. Regional integration initiatives and intra-African investments

Intense competition for markets and external resources provides a compelling reason why African countries should strengthen economic linkages among themselves through formal economic integration or through corporate integration. In their efforts to achieve expansion and rationalization of production capability and to acquire technology for industrial growth, policymakers in Africa should recognize the important role that TNCs from Africa and other developing countries could play to promote economic growth. The following recommendations are suggested in order to establish and strengthen corporate integration:

Policy recommendations

(a) Undertaking FDI projects on a regional basis

A strategic option by African TNCs, which are generally small, is to cooperate and invest with other firms based in other countries or in host economies.[43] The limited resources and skills make small firms extremely vulnerable in highly competitive markets. This explains why small transnationals have been more attracted to joint ventures in comparison to large transnationals. However, African governments' efforts to foster investment in viable regional projects that can exploit scale economies and counterbalance the potential monopolistic power of international TNCs are still wanting. There are many areas of possible collaboration among countries which could help to achieve this objective in the future. They include industrial collaboration agreements, licensing agreements, cooperation in engineering and technical services, training personnel, and rendering of research and development services. In this light, a more realistic approach to business-oriented investment and technology linkages among African countries is required at the firm level.

Cooperation should start with the identification and formulation of industrial projects of mutual interest, including the undertaking of feasibility studies and the formulation of bankable project proposals. Efficient information networks should be established to provide accurate and up-to-date information on investment opportunities, technological and market potential, national laws and regulations, costs, availability of labour and other inputs, potential partner experiences, etc. The development of industrial associations at the regional level could play a particularly stimulating role in linking local firms in different countries. Given Africa's infrastructural gap and its negative effect on regional integration, regional infrastructure projects are among the best candidates for these regional FDI projects. Moreover, given the importance of agriculture in most African economies, investment in the agricultural sector, both at the production and processing level, should form part of the development strategy at the regional level. These investments would preferably be greenfield investments in order to raise their very low level to at least the same level as M&As. In this regard, public–private partnerships could offer an interesting investment model given the complementarity of state and private sector actions combined with the enormity of the resources required to implement such projects.

(b) Deepening the regulatory measures to encourage intra-African FDI

Regulatory changes that occurred in the past two decades at the national level have deepened liberalization and deregulation which are expected to have a positive impact on FDI. In a survey of investment promotion agencies carried out in 2006, more than 90 per cent of African respondents stated that their policies targeted FDI from other developing countries, notably from within their own region (UNCTAD, 2006b). In Africa, South Africa tops the list of developing home countries targeted and this country also has an active strategy of involvement in regional investment schemes. The Industrial Development Corporation (IDC) and the Development Bank of Southern Africa are involved in, for example, equity financing of private sector projects in the Southern Africa region and elsewhere in Africa. In addition to participating directly in financing investments, IDC helps companies identify investment opportunities abroad. Furthermore, the Department of Trade and Industry has had some schemes aimed at supporting the internationalization of South Africa's automotive sector.[44]

To ensure that the interests of the business community are respected, its representation on national and regional policymaking bodies should be increased and made more systematic. Moreover, investment policies should be harmonized at the regional level to prevent conflicting objectives. To achieve this aim, there has to be balance between the role of micro (enterprises) and macro agents (governments and regional and international agencies) in the promotion of foreign investment in Africa.

(c) Encouraging regional rather than bilateral investment agreements

The strengthening of more limited initiatives on a bilateral basis should not preclude a region-wide approach to economic cooperation. African countries have tended to enter into more and more bilateral trade and investment agreements. By the end of 2007, Africa had concluded nearly 700 bilateral investment treaties, some 120 of which were with other African countries (UNCTAD, 2008f). However, bilateral schemes should eventually result in regional or multilateral schemes rather than vice versa. In order to attract more intra-African foreign investment, regional investment agreements are more effective than bilateral agreements. COMESA is a useful example of a regional bloc which is encouraging regional integration in the investment area.

Regional integration among countries at different levels of economic development may favour the more developed partners in terms of the distribution of the fruit of regional investment. To avoid this potential problem, home-host government incentives in directing investment flows and industrial development activities must take into account a sense of balance acceptable to all integrating parties.

(d) The need for a strong financial sector in Africa

The example of Nigerian banking reform has illustrated the need to have a solid financial sector in order to support a policy of intra-African investment. Indeed, the presence of banking networks in several African countries facilitates payment mechanisms needed to foster trade and financial flows across countries.

C. Strengthening regional trade in services and facilitating labour mobility and migration

Despite the provisions on trade in services found in regional integration treaties, implementation of these provisions and enforcement of commitments have fallen short of their intended objectives. The same applies to efforts by African countries to promote regional initiatives in trade facilitation. Regarding intra-African migration, it has been observed that strengthening and facilitating intra-African migration could be one of the important "deliverables" of regional integration agreements. Following are some recommendations:

1. Services trade

(a) Deepening openness in regional integration programmes

African countries have deepened regional economic integration by the inclusion of services in regional integration programmes. Consequently, there is a need to build on existing regional integration agreements treaties by including provisions that are relevant for the integration of services, such as the free movement of capital and labour, right of establishment and national treatment. For a more inclusive integration, the RECs should set up a mechanism for consultation with associations of trade in services providers, with a view to ensuring their involvement in the integration process of the region, increasing the intraregional FDI flows and boosting private sector development.

(b) Addressing the issues of barriers to services trade

At the national level, certain barriers to trade in services need to be removed or addressed to improve the conditions for services trade to flourish. These include (a) improving basic infrastructure such as transport, telecommunications and finance; (b) strengthening the private sector to encourage its involvement in the services sector and in trade in services; (c) enhancing the regulatory system, particularly those impacting on the supply and trade of services; and (d) addressing certain political barriers which impede the flourishing and expansion of services trade.

(c) Preparing to negotiate at the different levels of integration

African countries are engaged in services negotiations at different levels — i.e. within African RECs, between African RECs and external partners (such as the EU EPA), or individual African countries negotiating at WTO. Thus, it is important for these countries to engage in the necessary technical work to clearly identify their offensive and defensive interests and be clear on how they would want to see such interests crystallized in South–South regional RTAs, the North–South–South interregional context (EPAs), and the multilateral (WTO/GATS) level. There may be advantages and disadvantages with liberalization at the different levels, and it is important to determine which forum is likely to deliver the greatest gains on particular issues or sectors. Regional integration arrangements could be a way of building and enhancing competitiveness of industries and solidifying regulatory and institutional preparedness. Regional cooperation among contiguous states also provides opportunities for modernizing and expanding vital infrastructure networks such as roads, ports, railways and communications facilities, among others. North–South cooperation can benefit members through exploiting each other's complementarities. The multilateral level (WTO) offers more predictability, as obligations and commitments are carried out on a most-favoured-nation treatment basis, where all members are treated equally. There is also the possibility for dispute settlement and compensation to address non-compliance of obligations. The downside is that the process could drag on for years, bearing heavily on the already resource-constrained developing countries.

There is also the tendency in terms of making commitments — for trade liberalization — to always settle for the lowest common denominator. For these reasons, it is still beneficial to maintain regional integration arrangements, which can coexist alongside a country's membership in WTO.

(d) Promote the creation of large services firms

African countries should build on recent trends observed concerning the role of FDI in services activities — air transport, telecommunications and banking — in order to create a more dynamic and stronger services sector.

(e) Trade facilitation and regional integration should be tackled in a mutually-supported manner

Regional integration has enabled landlocked countries to become transit countries as a result of the intensification of intraregional trade flows. The RECs should accelerate their efforts aimed at harmonizing and improving transit/transport agreements in each subregion

2. Labour mobility and migration

(a) Implementing and enforcing provisions contained in the treaties

While all of the African RECs reviewed in this report contain provisions and protocols governing the free movement of people and the right of residence and establishment, most of these RECs maintain restrictions on the free flow of labour. There is thus a need to ensure that free flow of people, labour, and services, and the right of residence and establishment — as enshrined in the Abuja Treaty and the treaties of regional economic communities — are respected and implemented in various regional integration arrangements. It is acknowledged that countries in general are hesitant to open up their labour markets for various reasons, including security considerations, lack or absence of employment opportunities and competition for limited job openings. For this reason, a gradual and targeted approach to free flow of labour within RECs could be a more satisfactory option. This could mean providing for visa-free entry, the adoption of community travellers' cheques and passports (e.g. ECOWAS), among others. Members of RECs could also consider mechanisms to implement systematic recognition of qualifications and degrees obtained from other REC members. Another approach is to build on bilateral labour mobility agreements that already exist between and among contiguous states, and draw lessons which can be applied regionally.

(b) Building on the discussions and initiatives that are already in place with the aim of adopting a comprehensive labour mobility/migration policy at the regional level

It is encouraging that African governments, through the AU, have continued to engage themselves in discussions on migration, in particular on formulating policies that would maximize the developmental gains from migration for sending countries. Similarly, NEPAD's two-pronged approach to migration should be followed through as it deals with the question of retention of Africa's human resources by providing gainful employment, professional development and educational opportunities to qualified nationals in their home countries, and at the same time addressing the effects of brain drain by encouraging nationals abroad to contribute to the development of their country of origin through financial and human capital transfers.

(c) Complementing initiatives at the RECs with other cooperative inter-state and interregional approaches to labour mobility/ migration management

The ever-increasing number of labour movements, as well as other types of movement of people, leads to complexity in their management — thus, the need to develop, among others, a common migration policy among African countries towards harmonization of labour migration policies and the creation of regional approaches to labour migration issues. The regional consultative processes — which serve as a forum to exchange views on migration issues and the development of a common regional migration policy — are a step in the right direction and must be sustained, strengthened and replicated in other RECs. In addition, there is a need to strengthen intraregional and interregional cooperation and partnerships (including both South–South and South–North) to advance and systematize data collection and analysis on labour demand and supply in countries of origin and destination. Constituting a database on these migration issues could provide information needed for regular regional labour and migration exchanges and dialogue aimed at better matching labour demand and supply and, overall, better human resource development planning.

(d) National governments should play their part in supporting and complementing regional efforts to manage labour mobility at the regional level

National governments have the responsibility to provide both the foundation and supporting infrastructure to complement the efforts at the regional level. Labour mobility and migration at the intra-African level will only be as successful as the national governments want them to be. Governments should integrate and mainstream labour migration in national employment, labour market and development policy. This means instituting clear and transparent policies on migration that are linked to development strategies and national and regional programming (e.g. MDGs, Poverty Reduction Strategy Papers, TICAD) with the purpose of supporting economic and social development, including maximizing the benefits from migration. Migration management should likewise be prominent in the development agenda of governments so that the issue of brain drain is avoided, e.g. through advanced human resource planning, creating the necessary infrastructures for training and capacity-building and replenishment of needed skills and human resources. In this regard, it is key to set up reliable migration databases which are disaggregated by occupation, educational attainment, age and gender, among others.

(e) Ensuring that migration results in a win–win situation for countries in the region

There is a consensus that migration brings about net gains for both the home and host countries, but there are costs as well. The challenge is thus to ensure that gains are maximized and losses minimized. As remittances have been a major source of foreign earning for sending countries and have been linked to alleviating poverty and improving health and education outcomes in particular to the recipient families, mechanisms should be put in place to ensure that remittances are put into productive uses in the countries of origin and that remittance transfer costs are minimized. There are roles for all stakeholders in this regard, including the sending and receiving governments, the diaspora population, the migrants themselves, international organizations and civil society. Some best practices can be learned from earlier co-development initiatives undertaken by the French government with some North African sending countries, as well as with Senegal. Lessons can also be learned from the experiences of Spain and some Latin American sending countries, as well as Mexico's and Ecuador's policies of "matching funds" double or triple that of their country's remittance receipts. Instituting policies to retain talents or attract back and ensure the return of migrants could likewise benefit the continent. For example, it has been documented that there are skilled professionals from certain African countries who have chosen to move to other African countries rather than to the developed world.

D. Conclusion

The performance of regional integration arrangements in terms of trade, investment and migration reflects the evolution of the economic situation of the continent. The challenge is how to increase the developmental impact of regional integration in Africa. Regional integration is not an end in itself; it should be seen as a stepping stone towards Africa's attractiveness to investment and export competitiveness. The evolution of regional integration in Africa will be affected by the outcome of the Doha negotiations, which are intended to provide a new framework for the world trading system.

It will also be affected by the restructuring of the ACP–EU relations foreseen in the EPA negotiations, as well as the development of new bilateral economic relations, in particular with new emerging developing countries. African countries need to devise a new approach to regionalism which is better adapted to these realities.

Notes

1   One should not underestimate other non-economic objectives of integration, such as the need to establish closer political and cultural ties. However, these are not the focus of this chapter.

2   The effect of regionalism on accumulation is strongly associated with scale economies and network effects. A large economy makes large scale efficient and attracts a large number of firms. This can be beneficial for an economy when the scale of the firms and the networks they establish help them to lower production costs, making them more competitive.

3   It is only since a few years ago that these countries have been seriously rebuilding their EAC, widening it to include Burundi and Rwanda.

4   The discussion of empirical studies is presented later in the chapter.

5   See United States Department of State Trade and Investment Framework Agreements.

6   The popularity of this method does not mean that it is without problems. They evolve around the way the gravity model has been used, particularly in the context of estimating trade potential. Key among these problems is the heterogeneity of the sample used in terms of country composition and the exchange rate applied to estimate countries' gross domestic product (GDP); using current or purchasing power parity exchange rates leads to very different results (Fontagné et al, 2002). Despite these criticisms, the gravity model remains widely used in the analysis of international trade flows.

7   The effect on trade of belonging to a trading bloc is captured by dummy variables that are introduced into the gravity equation. These variables measure the average level of trade advantage for countries in a trade bloc relative to those not belonging to the trade bloc, controlling for other determinants of trade. Hence, when such a dummy variable is significant and positive (negative), the interpretation is that belonging to a trading bloc increases (decreases) the level of trade relative to a country outside the trade bloc. If the dummy variable turns out to be insignificant, its interpretation is that a trade bloc neither increases nor decreases a member country's level of trade.

8   See section 3 for details about the factors explaining these limited flows of intra-African trade.

9   These figures refer to officially recorded trade. They do not include informal cross-border trade among African countries, which could be substantial for some African countries. There are no reliable estimates that would allow for their inclusion. While this reduces the recorded levels of intra-African trade to some extent, it is not expected to substantially alter the picture depicted in this chapter.

10 It should be noted that, for some countries, particularly coastal ones with important regional port facilities, intra-African exports could comprise a sizable part of re-exports. However, we do not have the required data to determine the level of re-exports.

11 These figures refer to non-fuel exports to Africa as a proportion of total non-fuel exports. The comparative figures for total trade with Africa and sub-Saharan Africa are 8.7 per cent and 11.4 per cent, respectively.

12 Products listed at the SITC 3-digit level.

13   Collier and O'Connell (2008) test this hypothesis. They find that, globally, the hypothesis is indeed significant. Additional growth of one percentage point in a coastal economy can create up to 0.7 per cent growth in a neighbouring landlocked economy. Strikingly, Africa does not fit this global pattern. The likely explanation is that African landlocked economies have strong internal barriers to trade which isolate them further from regional markets.

14   Regional integration can be expected to change the size variables if economies are effectively integrated.

15   Studies of market integration in Africa have shown that, within countries, improvement in rural infrastructure, particularly roads, results in substantial increases in production and trade. In turn, these have a positive effect on household welfare and income growth (Dercon and Hoddinott, 2005).

16   Data from UNCTAD TRAINS database for 2006 shows that the unweighted average intra-African tariff rates on agricultural and industrial products were 9.03 per cent and 8.26 per cent, respectively. Within RTAs, tariffs are close to zero except for a few sensitive products. Hence, there is no evidence that high tariff rates are currently a major impediment to intra-African trade.

17   The limitations of the distance variable is due to a number of factors: (a) using the geodesic distance between two economic centres, as is normally the case, ignores the fact that trade routes do not necessarily follow a direct trajectory; (b) there are internal distances a product must cover before reaching a border (these are relatively easier to cover than external ones); (c) crossing a border usually involves additional costs such as delays and complying with administrative requirements, which adds to the "relative distance" a good has to cover before it reaches its market; and (d) location constraints can force a sub-optimal choice of a trading partner. For example, a landlocked country can be "forced" to trade with its neighbour even when this is not the most efficient choice (Fontagné et al, 2002).

18   Port efficiency has been found to be positively and significantly correlated with the levels of both imports and exports (Njinkeu et al., 2008).

19   Only 31 per cent of the road between Mali and Senegal is currently paved.

20   The index is calculated using the black market premium, FDI and an indicator of structural adjustment programmes.

21   At present, as much as two thirds of Africa's infrastructure spending is domestically resourced (Foster, 2008).

22   Why Burundi — and other African countries — trade less among themselves was discussed earlier.

23   These include the 1979–80 oil shock, the closure of the route to the sea due to the intensification of the war in Mozambique, the drought that ravaged agriculture production in 1979-80, the decline in terms of trade, and the drastic reduction in remittance flows from South Africa (for details, see Chipeta and Mkandawire, 2008).

24   Countries such as Mauritius and India are tapping into this growing market.

25   In the case of Ghana's interim EPA for example, this transitional period varies according to product categories between 5 and 15 years, with a category of sensitive products that is not subject to an obligation to liberalize.

26   Exports to the United States are dominated by oil but non-oil products also increased remarkably over the period. Non-oil exports were $3.4 billion in 2007, twice the

2001 amount. The list of non-oil exports includes apparel, footwear, vehicles, fruits and nuts, prepared vegetables, leather products, cut flowers, prepared seafood, and essential oils.

27 The "abundant supply" provision restricted the use by an apparel manufacturer of fabrics originating from non-AGOA countries. The need to comply with this provision had created uncertainty among United States apparel importers. The repeal is expected to boost United States apparel imports from suppliers in 12 African countries.

28 Information from http://www.ustr.gov/Trade_Agreements/TIFA/Section_Index.html accessed on 29 January 2009.

29 The level of FDI from Africa to small African economies may well be understated in official FDI data, as a significant proportion of such investment goes to their informal sector, which is not included in government statistics.

30 Foreign investment is the cause of some friction in parts of Africa. In Southern Africa, for example, the dominance of South Africa raises some concerns in some quarters. These are fuelled by the feeling that South African competition could drive domestic firms out of the market. Some consider that unfair competition could be at play, the reason why countries such as Mauritius and Zambia have been requesting more market access in South Africa, particularly for their textiles and apparels (Odenthal, 2001).

31 The importance of South Africa would be even higher if some big formerly South African firms such as South African Breweries and De Beers with interests across Africa were not now listed offshore.

32 Such investments were mainly made by foreign companies operating in Mauritius.

33 In countries where land is not privately owned, and there are many in Africa, it is difficult to encourage domestic and foreign private investment in agriculture.

34 The bank compiles the country's balance of payments according to the International Monetary Fund Balance of Payments Manual (Revision 5).

35 Due to data limitations, some African countries either do not report investment flows into other countries or have insignificant levels of investment on South Africa's balance of payments account. Such countries are recorded under the category "rest of Africa"; they comprise 30 African countries which together account for less than 10 per cent of South Africa's stock of foreign investment. Consequently, there are six subregions in the destination analysis.

36 One United States dollar is currently valued at 10.40 rand.

37 The public sector comprises public authorities and public corporations; these entities do not invest outside their subregion, according to the dataset, hence analysis of the public sector is omitted.

38 In February 2009, WTO had registered 160 RTAs worldwide, of which 60 had services coverage.

39 See COMESA Strategy.

40 In recent years, the phenomenon of international migration has grown in importance and has been afforded high-profile attention, above all by the United Nations, with the convening of the Global Commission on International Migration in 2005, comprising high-level migration experts and practitioners. The report of the commission was to serve as the strategic guide for governments on the issue of international migration. In 2007, the United Nations organized the High-level Dialogue on International Migration and Development in 2007 and the community of states has henceforth continued the

discussions on international migration through the Global Forum on Migration and Development, which had its inaugural meeting in Brussels in July 2007 and the second meeting in Manila in October 2008.

41   It must be noted that, in the context of the General Agreement of Trade in Services (GATS), the term used is temporary movement of service providers, or Mode 4 of providing services.

42   ICA was launched in 2005. Its mission is to support the scaling up of investment for infrastructure development in Africa from both public and private sources. It also seeks to help remove some of the technical and political challenges to building more infrastructure and to better coordinate activities of its members and other significant sources of infrastructure finance (e.g. China, India and Arab countries). Its members are G-8 countries, the World Bank, the African Development Bank, the European Commission, the European Investment Bank, and the Development Bank of Southern Africa.

43   Not surprisingly, the incidence of joint venture arrangements, equity and non-equity, among TNCs from developing countries is quite high.

44   UNCTAD, "Emerging FDI from developing countries", note prepared by the UNCTAD secretariat at the Commission on Investment, Technology and Related Financial Flows, ninth session, Geneva, 7–11 March 2005.

References

Adedeji A (2002). History and prospects for regional integration in Africa. Paper presented at the Third Meeting of the African Development Forum, Addis Ababa, Ethiopia. 3–8 March.

African Business (2008a). Africa-wide pool of winners scoops the 2nd African Banker. *African Business*. November: 47.

African Business (2008b). Les 100 premières banques d'Afrique 2008: Classement annuel d'African Business. *African Business Edition Française*, November/December: 6–25.

African Union (2008). Addis Ababa Declaration on EPA Negotiations, AU/EXP/CAMTF/ Decl. (I), Conference of Ministers of Trade and Finance, 1–3 April.

Amjadi A and Yeats A (1995). Have transport costs contributed to the relative decline of sub-Saharan African exports? Some preliminary empirical evidence. Policy Research Working Paper 1559. Washington DC: World Bank.

Asiedu E (2002). On the determinants of foreign direct investment to developing countries: Is Africa different? *World Development*, 30 (1): 107–119.

Atingi-Ego M and Kasekende L (2008). Uganda: growth in a post-conflict economy, in Ndulu B, O'Connell S, Azam J-P, Bates RH, Fosu AK, Gunning JW and Njinkeu D (eds.), *The Political Economy of Economic Growth in Africa, 1960-2000*. Cambridge University Press, 244–285.

Baldwin RE (1997). Review of theoretical developments on regional integration, in Oyejide A, Elbadawi I and Collier P (eds.) *Regional Integration and Trade Liberalization in sub-Saharan Africa*. Volume 1: Framework, Issues and Methodological Perspectives. London: Macmillan Press Ltd: 24–88.

Buys P, Deichmann U and Wheeler D (2006). Road network upgrading and overland trade expansion in sub-Saharan Africa. World Bank Policy Research Working Paper 4097. Washington DC: World Bank.

Cernat L (2001). Assessing regional trade arrangements: Are South–South RTAs more trade diverting? in *Policy Issues in International Trade and Commodities Study Series*, No. 16. UNCTAD, New York and Geneva.

Chipeta C and Mkandawire M (2008). Man-made opportunities and growth, in Ndulu B, O'Connell S, Azam J-P, Bates RH, Fosu AK, Gunning JW and Njinkeu D (eds.), *The Political Economy of Economic Growth in Africa, 1960–2000*, 2: 143–165. Cambridge University Press.

Collier P and O'Connell S (2008). Opportunities and choices, in Ndulu B, O'Connell S, Bates RH, Collier P and Soludo C (eds.), *The Political Economy of Economic Growth in Africa, 1960–2000*. 1:76-136. Cambridge University Press.

Corden M (1972). Economies of scale and customs union theory. *Journal of Political Economy*. 80 (3): 465–475.

Coulibaly S and Fontagné L (2005). South–South trade: geography matters. *Journal of African Economies*. 15 (2): 313–341.

Dercon S and Hoddinott J (2005). *Livelihoods, growth and links to market towns in 15 Ethiopian villages*. FCND Discussion Paper 194. International Food Policy Research Institute, Washington DC.

Dinka T and Kennes W (2007). Africa's regional integration arrangements: history and challenges. European Centre for Development Policy Management. Discussion Paper No. 74.

Ecobank (2009). *Our Group.* Available at http://www.ecobank.com/.

ECA (2004). *Assessing Regional Integration in Africa: ECA Policy Research Report.* Addis Ababa: ECA.

ECA (2006a). *Assessing Regional Integration in Africa II: Rationalizing Regional Economic Communities.* Addis Ababa: ECA.

ECA (2006b), *International Migration and Development: Implications for Africa.* Addis Ababa: ECA.

ECA (2008). *Assessing Regional Integration in Africa III: Towards Monetary and Financial Integration in Africa.* Addis Ababa: ECA.

Elbadawi I (1997). The impact of regional trade and monetary schemes on intra-sub-Saharan Africa trade in Oyejide A, Elbadawi I and Collier P (eds.), *Regional Integration and Trade Liberalization in sub-Saharan Africa.* Volume 1: Framework, Issues and Methodological Perspectives. London: Macmillan Press Ltd: 210–255.

Fafchamps M, Gunning JW and Oostendorp R (2000). Inventories and risk in African manufacturing. *Economic Journal,* 110 (466): 861–893.

Fink C and Jansen M (2007). Services provision in regional trade agreements: Stumbling or building blocks for multilateral liberalization? Paper presented at the Conference on Multilateralizing Regionalism, Geneva, Switzerland, 10–12 September.

Fontagné L, Pajot M and Pasteels J-M (2002). Potentiels de commerce entre économies hétérogènes: un petit mode d'emploi des modèles de gravité. *Économie et Prévision,* 152–153 (1–2): 115–139.

Foroutan F and Pritchett L (1993). Intra-sub-Saharan African trade: is it too little? World Bank Policy Research Working Paper 1225. Washington DC: World Bank.

Foster V (2008). Overhauling the engine of growth: infrastructure in Africa. *Africa Infrastructure Country Diagnostic.* Executive Summary, The World Bank, Washington, DC.

Gad M (2009). A better future for Africa: recommendations from the private sector. Paper prepared for the Africa Commission. Copenhagen: Confederation of Danish Industry.

Gbetnkom D (2008). Is South–South regionalism always a diversion? Empirical evidence from CEMAC. *International Trade Journal,* 22 (1): 85–112.

Himbara D (1994). *Kenyan Capitalists, the State and Development.* Boulder: Lynne Rienner and Publishers.

ICTSD (2008). Three African Trade Blocs to Merge. *Bridges,* 12(5) November 2008.

IOM (2005). *World Migration 2005.* Geneva: IOM.

IOM (2008). *World Migration 2008.* Geneva: IOM.

Iraqi F (2007). Le Maroc à la Conquête de l'Afrique, *Tel Quel* [Online], 20–26 janvier. Available at http://www.telquel-online.com/257/economie1_257.shtml.

Krugman PR (1991). *Geography and Trade.* Cambridge, MA: MIT Press.

Limao N and Venables AJ (2001). Infrastructure, geographical disadvantage and transport costs. *World Bank Economic Review.* 15 (3): 451–479.

Little PD (2007). Unofficial Cross-Border Trade in Eastern Africa. Paper presented at the FAO workshop on "Staple Food Trade and Market Policy Options for Promoting Development in Eastern and Southern Africa," Rome, 1–2 March.

Longo R and Sekkat K (2004). Economic obstacles to expanding intra-African trade. *World Development*. 32 (8): 1309–1321.

Metzger M (2008). *Regional cooperation and integration in sub-Saharan Africa.* UNCTAD Discussion Paper 189. Geneva: UNCTAD.

Milner C, Morrissey O and Zgovu E (2008). Trade facilitation in developing countries. CREDIT Research Paper 08/05. Centre for Research in Economic Development and International Trade, University of Nottingham.

Muwanga D (2009). Africa: United Republic of Tanzania, Rwanda, Burundi Seal Railway Deal. *The New Vision*. Uganda. published on 27 January.

Mwega FM and Ndung'u N (2008). Explaining African economic growth performance: The case of Kenya. In Ndulu, B., O'Connell, S.A. (eds). *The Political Economy*.

Ndikumana L and Verick S (2008). The linkages between FDI and domestic investment: unraveling the developmental impact of foreign investment in sub-Saharan Africa. *Development Policy Review*, 26 (6): 713–726.

Ndulu B (2006). Infrastructure, regional integration and growth in sub-Saharan Africa: dealing with the disadvantages of geography and sovereign fragmentation. *Journal of African Economies*. AERC Supplement 2: 212–244.

Ndulu B, O'Connell SA, Azam JT, Bates RH, Fosu AK, Gunning JW and Njinkeu D (eds.) (2008). *The Political Economy of Economic Growth in Africa, 1960–2000*. Volume 2, Country Case Studies. Cambridge University Press.

NEPAD (2006). *An Indicative Assessment to Determine Prospects for a NEPAD Spatial Development Programme*. Regional SDI Programme Support Unit & MINTEK.

Njinkeu D and Powo Fosso B (2006). Intra-African trade and regional integration. Paper prepared for the ADB/AERC International Conference on Accelerating Africa's Development Five Years into the Twenty-first Century. Tunis. 22–24 November.

Njinkeu D, Wilson J and Powo Fosso B (2008). Expanding trade within Africa: the impact of trade facilitation. World Bank Policy Research Working Paper 4790. Washington DC: World Bank.

Nkurunziza JD and Ngaruko F (2008). Why has Burundi grown so slowly? in Ndulu B, O'Connell SA, Azam JT, Bates RH, Fosu AK, Gunning JW and Njinkeu D (eds.) *The Political Economy of Economic Growth in Africa, 1960–2000*, Volume 2, Country Case Studies. Cambridge University Press: 51–85.

Nordas HK (2001). South Africa: A developing country and net outward investor. Working Paper No. 20/01. Foundation for Research in Economics and Business Administration, Bergen.

Olubomehin D and Kawonishe D (2004). The African Union and the challenges of regional integration in Africa. Paper submitted to the annual conference of the African Studies Association of Australia and the Pacific (AFSAAP). 26–28 November. University of Western Australia.

Odenthal L (2001). FDI in sub-Saharan Africa. Research programme on integration and cooperation in sub-Saharan Africa. Working Paper No. 173. OECD Development Centre.

Office of the United States Trade Representative (2008). *2008 Comprehensive Report on United States Trade and Investment Policy toward sub-Saharan Africa and Implementation of the African Growth and Opportunity Act*. Washington DC.

Onwuamaeze D (2008). Looking Beyond Nigeria. *Newswatch Magazine*. 7 October. Available at http://www.newswatchngr.com,

Oyejide TA (2005). Trade liberalization, regional integration and African development in the context of structural adjustment, IDRC/CRDI.

Oyejide A, Elbadawi I and Collier P (eds.) (1997). *Regional Integration and Trade Liberalization in sub-Saharan Africa*. Volume 1: Framework, Issues and Methodological Perspectives. London: Macmillan Press Ltd.

Portugal-Perez A and Wilson J (2008). Trade costs in Africa: barriers and opportunities for reform. World Bank Policy Research Working Paper 4619. Washington DC: World Bank.

Schiff M (1997). Small is beautiful: Preferential trade agreements and the impact of country size, market share and smuggling. *Journal of Economic Integration*. 12 (3): 359–387.

Shaw W (2007). Migration in Africa: A review of the economic literature on international migration in 10 countries. Discussion Paper 43096, Washington DC: World Bank.

Sheridan M (2007). China builds African empire. *Times Online*. Accessed at: http://business.timesonline.co.uk/tol/business/markets/china/article2889489.ece.

South Centre (2008). EPAs and Development Assistance: rebalancing rights and obligations. South Centre Fact Sheet No. 12. Geneva: South Centre.

United Nations (2004). *World Economic and Social Survey 2004*. United Nations publication, sales No. E.04.II.F.20, New York and Geneva.

UNCTAD (2006a). *Review of Maritime Transport 2006*. United Nations publication, sales No. E.06.II.D.7, New York and Geneva.

UNCTAD (2006b). *World Investment Report 2006: FDI from Developing and Transition Economies: Implications for Development*. United Nations publication, sale No. E.06.II.D.11, New York and Geneva.

UNCTAD (2007a). Regional cooperation in transit transport: Solutions for landlocked and transit developing countries. TD/B/COM.3/EM.30/2. Note by the UNCTAD secretariat. Trade and Development Board, Commission on Enterprise, Business Facilitation and Development, Expert meeting on regional cooperation in transit transport: Solutions for landlocked and transit developing countries. Geneva, 27–28 September 2007.

UNCTAD (2007b). Trade in services and development implications. Trade and Development Board. Commission on Trade in Goods and Services, and Commodities. Eleventh session. Geneva, 19–23 March. Item 4 of the provisional agenda.

UNCTAD (2007c). *Trade and Development Report 2007*. United Nations publication, sales No. E.07.II.D.11, New York and Geneva.

UNCTAD (2008a). *Economic Development in Africa: Export Performance Following Trade Liberalization — Some Patterns and Policy Perspectives*. United Nations publication, sales No. E.08.II.D.22, New York and Geneva.

UNCTAD (2008b). Foreign direct investment in landlocked countries: Trends, policies and the way forward. UNCTAD/ALDC/2008/43, Geneva and New York.

UNCTAD (2008c). *Handbook of Statistics*. Available online at http://www.unctad.org/.

UNCTAD (2008d). *Information Economy Report 2007-2008*. Science and technology for development: the new paradigm of ICT. United Nations publication, sales No. E.07.II.D.13, New York and Geneva.

UNCTAD (2008e). *Review of Maritime Transport 2008*. Special Chapter: Latin America and the Caribbean. Geneva. United Nations publication, sales No. E.08.II.D.26, New York and Geneva.

UNCTAD (2008f). *World Investment Directory: Volume X*. United Nations publication, Sales No. E.08.II.D.3, New York and Geneva.

UNCTAD (2008g). *World Investment Report 2008: Transnational Corporations and the Infrastructure Challenge*. United Nations publication, sales No. E.08.II.D.23, New York and Geneva.

UNCTAD (2009). South–South cooperation and regional cooperation: Where we stand and future directions. Note by the Secretariat for the Trade and Development Board, Investment, Enterprise and Development Commission. Multi-year expert meeting on investment cooperation: South-South Cooperation and regional integration. 4–5 February, Geneva.

Viner J (1950). *The Customs Union Issue*. Washington, DC, Carnegie Endowment for International Peace.

Wade A (2008). Maroc-Senegal, un flux d'affaire croissant, mais à sens unique. *Les Afriques* [Online], 11 juillet. Available at http://www.lesafriques.com.

Whitaker Group (2008). *Lesotho Update*. A Whitaker Group Publication, Fall.

World Bank (2000). *Trade Blocs*. New York: Oxford University Press.

World Bank (2008). *Migration and Remittance Factbook 2008*. Washington DC: World Bank.

World Bank (2009). *Doing Business Database*. Available online at http://www.worldbank.org.

Yeats A (1998). What can be expected from African regional trade arrangements? Some empirical evidence. Policy Research Working Paper 2004, Washington DC: World Bank.

Economic Development in Africa series:

2000   *Capital Flows and Growth in Africa* –TD/B/47/4–UNCTAD/GDS/MDPB/7
Contributors: Yilmaz Akyüz, Kamran Kousari (team leader), Korkut Boratav (consultant).

2001   *Performance, Prospects and Policy Issues*–UNCTAD/GDS/AFRICA/1
Contributors: Yilmaz Akyüz, Kamran Kousari (team leader), Korkut Boratav (consultant).

2002   *From Adjustment to Poverty Reduction:What is New?*–UNCTAD/GDS/AFRICA/2
Contributors: Yilmaz Akyüz, Kamran Kousari (team leader), Korkut Boratav (consultant).

2003   *Trade Performance and Commodity Dependence* – UNCTAD/GDS/AFRICA/2003/1
Contributors: Yilmaz Akyüz, Kamran Kousari (team leader), Samuel Gayi.

2004   *Debt Sustainability: Oasis or Mirage?* – UNCTAD/GDS/AFRICA/2004/1
Contributors: Kamran Kousari (team leader), Samuel Gayi, Bernhard Gunter (consultant), Phillip Cobbina (research).

2005   *Rethinking the Role of Foreign Direct Investment* – UNCTAD/GDS/AFRICA/2005/1
Contributors: Kamran Kousari (team leader), Samuel Gayi, Richard Kozul-Wright, Phillip Cobbina (research).

2006   *Doubling Aid: Making the "Big Push" Work* – UNCTAD/GDS/AFRICA/2006/1
Contributors: Kamran Kousari (team leader), Samuel Gayi, Richard Kozul-Wright, Jane Harrigan (consultant), Victoria Chisala (research).

2007   *Reclaiming Policy Space: Domestic Resource Mobilization and Developmental States* – UNCTAD/ALDC/AFRICA/2007
Contributors: Samuel Gayi (team leader), Janvier Nkurunziza, Martin Halle, Shigehisa Kasahara.

2008   *Export Performance Following Trade Liberalization: Some Patterns and Policy Perspectives* - UNCTAD/ALDC/AFRICA/2008
Contributors: Samuel Gayi (team leader), Janvier Nkurunziza, Martin Halle, Shigehisa Kasahara.

Copies of the series of reports on *Economic Development in Africa* may be obtained from the Division for Africa, Least Developed Countries and Special Programmes, UNCTAD, Palais des Nations, CH-1211 Geneva 10, Switzerland (fax: 022 917 0274; e-mail: africadev@unctad.org). The reports are also accessible on the UNCTAD website at www.unctad.org/Africa/series